THE DRAMATURGY OF
SHAKESPEARE'S ROMANCES

The Dramaturgy of
Shakespeare's Romances

BARBARA A. MOWAT

THE UNIVERSITY OF GEORGIA PRESS
ATHENS

Library of Congress Catalog Card Number: 75–21177
International Standard Book Number: 0–8203–0389–5

The University of Georgia Press, Athens 30602

Set in 12 on 15 pt. Intertype Garamond type
Printed in the United States of America

TO THE MEMORY OF
Robert David Saltz

Contents

Acknowledgments

Parts of this book have appeared as articles published in *Shakespeare Quarterly* and *Renaissance Papers*. I gratefully acknowledge the permission to reprint granted me by the editors of these publications.

My obligations to others are many. It is a pleasure to thank, first of all, Fredson Bowers and Robert Langbaum, who first encouraged me to write about the dramaturgy of Shakespeare's romances. From Jack D. Durant, Ward Allen, Norman Brittin, and Eugene Current-Garcia, I have received invaluable support and guidance. John Meagher, Wolfgang Iser, and Howard Felperin generously shared their time and their insights at crucial points in the writing. And David K. Jeffrey has been unfailingly supportive; my gratitude to him is immense.

Special thanks are due to Rob Howe and David Bjurberg, for helpful criticism of the manuscript; to Janie Rahman, who typed successive drafts with patience and care; to the staffs of the Folger Shakespeare Library, the Newberry Library, and the Auburn University Library; and to my children, Bill and Beth, who have been patient with me.

THE DRAMATURGY OF
SHAKESPEARE'S ROMANCES

Prologue

When I first read, many years ago, the opening lines of *The Winter's Tale:* "If you shall chance, Camillo, to visit Bohemia, on the like occasion whereon my services are now on foot," I realized that I had unwittingly stepped into a strange new world. Here was Shakespeare, but Shakespeare with a difference. And, as I moved through the play, the familiar Shakespearean landmarks—the divisions between husband and wife, father and child, ruler and counselor; the storm, the clown; the reunions and recognitions; the wonderfully resonant images—served only to make the strangeness of the landscape the more haunting. Bears eating men who cry out, as they are eaten, that they are noblemen? Choruses who announce in rhymed couplets that the play we are watching is already staled by time? Statues which come to life? Language so thick with the pressure of passion that it bursts beyond coherence? What, I kept asking, was Shakespeare doing? And when I turned to *Cymbeline* and *The Tempest*, the question remained, persistent and unanswered; these plays, too, were strange—hauntingly Shakespearean, rich with familiar themes, familiar characters, familiar motifs—yet in them, as in *The Winter's Tale*, everything Shakespearean had undergone fantastic transformations. The strangeness in these plays, I felt, could not be accidental, nor the result of Shakespeare's boredom, inexpertness, or senility. In the strangeness was a pattern, could one but find it.

The following pages are the result of my attempts to find that pattern. In my search I have set severe limits, tied myself to a few key questions, and have made several assumptions. I have, for example, concerned myself almost solely with the way the plays are made, and have dealt with themes and meanings only tangentially: we all know, as Philip Edwards put it, that in these plays "something important is being said"[1]—but every account that I have read that has attempted to reduce the plays to thematic statement, to express what they say in words other than the words of the plays themselves, has, indeed, *reduced* the plays. Rich with meaning, these plays reveal that meaning to us only through the experience of the play as a whole, or through glimpses, fragments, or lines and images which haunt us. The flame of meaning is there, but we may not approach it directly: like Spenser's Calidore who would see the Graces dancing, we move toward the central mystery only to have it disappear at our approach. Not only do these plays say too much, too complexly, ever to submit gracefully to restatement, but also in these plays, more than in any other Shakespearean drama, the meanings are so intricately connected with the form that an understanding of the form is an essential first step toward an understanding of the plays: hence my concentration on Shakespeare's *poesis* in the Romances.

Again, I have limited myself to the three Romances which are now unhesitatingly accepted as Shakespeare's own work. It is with regret that I almost bypass *Pericles:* much that I have discovered about *Cymbeline, The Winter's Tale,* and *The Tempest* is obviously applicable to this "experiment in Jacobean processional drama" (to use Northrop Frye's descriptive phrase).[2] But, for me, the authorship-textual problem of *Pericles* is yet a problem,[3] and since my concern is with authentic Shakespearean strangeness, I discuss *Pericles* only briefly, and *Henry VIII* and *Two Noble Kinsmen* not at all.

As for my assumptions: first, I assume a close connection between Shakespeare's Romances and the basic Greek Romance form, this in spite of the fact that the connection remains to be firmly established.[4] The history of Greek Romance and its influence on medieval saints' legends and on miracle plays based on saints' legends makes the problem of proving direct influence almost impossible; any unsympathetic critic can simply point to intermediate medieval sources or to Renaissance forms influenced by Greek Romance: romantic epics, Italian novella, Elizabethan prose romances, the *Arcadia*, or the *Faerie Queene*—and say, justly, that one cannot prove direct influence on Shakespeare's Romances by Achilles Tatius or Heliodorus. This I grant. Yet I maintain that if we do not recognize the close kinship between Shakespeare's Romances and the world of Greek Romance, we are in serious danger of misunderstanding the plays. This is especially true when we attempt to assess the tone of the Romances: there is a kind of seriousness, of piety, if you will, in the medieval and Renaissance versions of Greek Romance not to be found in such works as *Clitophon and Leucippe* or the *Aethiopica*, and not to be found, I maintain, in Shakespeare's Romances.

My second assumption is that the text of the plays gives us the clues we need in order to understand their form and their expected response. Thus, although studies of performances of the Romances, of their stage histories, or of the kinds of audiences the plays doubtless had at their early performances would undoubtedly be useful, investigations of performance problems or of Jacobean social history have proved, for me, to be intriguing byways that lead away from more compelling questions. For me, Kenneth Burke's conception of literary form and its control of audience response is central: I believe, with Burke, that when an author chooses a story, a genre, a theatrical style, a narrative or a dramatic mode, he is choosing a way of creating a certain kind of experience and a way of saying what he wants to say.[5] This assumption has been important in guiding my thinking, and will become a part of my argument in the later pages of my study.

My third assumption is that there is some merit in considering these three plays as a group. This is, I know, a debatable assumption, and I am aware that each play is unique and should eventually be considered and responded to in its own uniqueness. Yet it is necessary to see the ways in which the plays are dramaturgically alike and, as a group, distinct from Shakespeare's other plays, before we can come to terms with the plays individually. Hence my approach has been more collective than individual, with each chapter concentrating on a dramaturgical issue rather than on a particular play (though each chapter does, in fact, use one play as its primary focus of study). The first chapter considers comedy and tragedy in the Romances, putting most of its stress on *The Winter's Tale*, where the two genres are most shockingly and obviously conjoined; the second chapter deals with theatrical tactics and theatrical styles, emphasizing *Cymbeline* because, of all the Romances, *Cymbeline* has been most open to attack or apology because of its "primitive"—or, as they are now called, "artificial"—tactics. The third chapter on narrative and dramatic modes gives extra attention to *The Tempest*. The final chapters, by pointing the connections between the questions asked and answered in earlier chapters, trace out the dramaturgical pattern which informs the three plays—the pattern which determines and explains their strangeness.

It will be clear to all scholars who work with the Romances that this book is an attempt to answer Philip Edwards's plea that we try to look closely at the Romances to determine, first, just what Shakespeare was doing when he wrote these plays, and, second, how we should respond to them.[6] My hope is that by trying to answer a few central questions, I have made some headway toward clearing the critical ground for sensitive, authentic responses to these wonderful creations.

CHAPTER I

"Doleful Matter Merrily Set Down": Tragedy and Comedy in the Romances

The indefinably odd quality which some commentators have found in the "late comedies" may perhaps be attributed to Shakespeare's placing events ordinarily suggestive of the tragic mode into the framework of a closed system, the domain of the comic spirit. Was he trying to write tragedy from God's viewpoint instead of from man's?

—Herbert McArthur[1]

"Doleful matter merrily set down": the words are the Clown's in *The Winter's Tale*, his description of the kind of ballad he likes.[2] But his words point beyond Autolycus's ballads to *The Winter's Tale* itself, and to *Cymbeline* and *The Tempest* as well. Strange blends of dolor and mirth, Shakespeare's Romances remind us here of *Othello*, there of *As You Like It;* refusing generic classification, they tantalize the critic who would place them, if he only could, *somewhere.* "Doleful matter": why, then, not place them with the tragedies, as expansions of Shakespeare's tragic form? Or, since they are "merrily set down," and do, indeed, have joyful endings, why not link them to the comedies? Many critics have, of course, done so.[3] Or why not admit their "generic ambiguity,"[4] label them "tragicomedies," and turn one's critical attention to more important matters?

It is easy to scoff at the critic who would, at this date, continue to puzzle his mind with the tragedy-comedy problem in Shakespeare's Romances. Attempts to classify plays generically are, *prima facie,* suspect; further, "romance" has by now become an almost sacrosanct word, one that carries with it its own special otherworldly tonality. Yet if we look closely at the plays, we realize anew that in them

5

Shakespeare blends dole and mirth most strangely and that in the blending lie questions that beg for answers.

In order to locate these questions, let us begin by examining earlier attempts to place the Romances inside the bounds of traditional Shakespearean genres. Some critics have suggested—E. M. W. Tillyard among them—that we locate the plays at the further reaches of Shakespearean tragedy. Tillyard's argument is both persuasive and influential.[5] He argues that the complete tragic vision moves beyond destruction to reconciliation and regeneration, and suggests that Shakespeare, in his last plays, went beyond the destructive phase of tragedy explored in such master works as *Othello* and *King Lear*. In *Cymbeline, The Winter's Tale*, and *The Tempest*, says Tillyard, Shakespeare "added his *Eumenides* to the already completed *Agamemnon* and *Choephori*." Tillyard grants that in the last plays are strange conjunctions of tragedy and comedy, but these conjunctions, he feels, are merely signs of Shakespeare's greatness and of the breadth of his tragic vision.

The attraction of Tillyard's argument lies in its recognition of the destructive elements which certainly appear in these plays, in its focusing of our attention on those tragic patterns which are embedded in them, and in its linking of the plays to Shakespeare's great tragedies. Those critics who view the plays as dramatized allegory or symbol, who discuss them in terms of vegetation rite, primitive myth, or "lesser incarnations of the Christ figure,"[6] are particularly drawn to Tillyard's argument, for if the plays are indeed the final development of Shakespeare's tragic vision, then profound meanings are certainly to be sought for and found in them.

Yet Tillyard's argument ignores certain disturbing facts about the Romances. He maintains, for example (and this is a crucial point in his general thesis), that the first part of *The Winter's Tale* renders worthily the "destructive phase" of tragedy before moving into the "good earthy comedy" of the second part. Tillyard defines the destructive phase of tragedy in the accepted Aristotelian-Hegelian-Bradleian tradition, with emphasis on the tragic hero, on conflict, suffering, and a sense of universality. In this phase (the phase which, according to Tillyard, Shakespeare explores in his major tragedies) "man . . . at his highest . . . is summoned to resist certain things in the universal scheme and suffering and loss result."[7] Such a definition will do as an approximation for what happens in *Othello;* but I maintain that it is not seriously applicable to the "destructive phase" of *The Winter's Tale.*

Tillyard is right in noting that the first part of *The Winter's Tale* appears to represent "in full view of the audience" a true Shakespearean tragedy.[8] Here, a king, through mad jealousy, cruelly accuses his virtuous wife of adultery and treason, attempts to murder a fellow king, and sentences his infant daughter to certain death. At the end of the "tragic" section, the king's son is dead, his wife and daughter appear to be dead, and the king is left in grief-stricken repentance. Yet this is merely the plot outline of the "destructive phase" of *The Winter's Tale.* And critics who have assumed from this outline that Shakespeare intended the story to be tragic, who have judged it by "rules of tragic workmanship," have found that, as tragedy, it "presents flagrant specimens of inferior artistry."[9] Noting the resemblance between *Othello* and Leontes' story, such critics have commented upon the inferiority of the tragedy in *The Winter's Tale* without examining the major differences in Shakespeare's handling of the parallel fables that underlie *Othello* and *The Winter's Tale.*[10] Such an examination is highly instructive if we are to understand why the Romances are seen incorrectly when seen as "expanded Shakespearian tragedy." Since even Tillyard admits that only in *The Winter's Tale* is "the destructive phase of tragedy" presented fully— *Cymbeline* he considers an unsuccessful attempt to present the complete tragic vision, and *The Tempest* he recognizes as a play which focuses totally on "the regenerative phase"—what we discover about Shakespeare's methods of handling tragic material in *The Winter's Tale* will apply with even greater force to these two "less tragic" plays.

Let us for the moment consider the "destructive phase" of *The Winter's Tale* as a complete play—a dangerous procedure, but one partially justified by the numerous references to it as an autonomous tragedy. When we look at this "play"—which, for simplicity's sake, we will call "the Leontes-story"—we find that it (like *Cymbeline*) is indeed strikingly similar to *Othello*. The plot turns on the husband's unjustified jealousy of suspected adultery between his virtuous wife and best friend, and includes the attempted murder of the friend and the death of the wife—"I say she's dead; I'll swear it." Beyond this obvious plot-similarity are also significant parallels in the casts of characters, in the movement of the actions, and in many important speeches and key scenes. Note, for instance, the denouement scene in the two plays (*Othello* 5.2; *Winter's Tale* 3.2), each opening with the husband determined to bring about his wife's death, closing with his grief and repentance; each including similar exhortations to confession, protestations of innocence, and violent outbursts from the loyal companion Emilia/Paulina. Such parallels occur in many scenes of the plays.

Yet *Othello* is tragedy, "the Leontes-story" is not. When we consider the basic fable which Shakespeare worked with in the two plays, we should wonder more at the first assertion than at the second, for the story around which both plays are written is melodramatic and lurid—a story of adultery, revenge, and murder not unlike the actual sordid events reported in the scandal sheets of the day[11] and dramatized in such domestic "tragedies" as *Arden of Fe-*

versham (1592). Yet by making subtle but significant changes in the source story of *Othello* (a tale in Cinthio's *Hecatommithi,* 1565), Shakespeare "pierced beneath the plot" of lurid domestic melodrama and converted it into high tragedy.[12]

In the first place, as H. B. Charlton notes, Shakespeare adds to the Moor's story a scene in which Othello and Desdemona describe to the senators the nature and development of their love, converting the few inert lines about the Moor's wooing of Desdemona in Cinthio into a powerful statement about the marriage of true minds. In the second place he alters the character of "the Ensign" in such a way that, in place of a military man motivated solely by sexual jealousy, we have Iago, a character so evil that, through him, larger-than-human forces seem to enter the play and operate against Othello. Third, Shakespeare makes Othello of noble descent, and of a deeply religious nature. All of these changes lead to such a general ennobling of Othello's character that he can, indeed, represent "man at his highest." As Charlton suggests, contrast Othello's "solemn sacrifice" of Desdemona with the crude slaughter of her counterpart in Cinthio, and one sees immediately that Cinthio's Moor and Shakespeare's Othello belong to two different human kinds.

Note now the way in which Shakespeare treats Greene's *Pandosto* (1588) in shaping "the Leontes-story." Here, instead of emphasizing the love between Leontes and Hermione, he passes over Greene's account of "these two, linked together in perfect love,"[13] and has Leontes summarize his courtship in the curt lines: "Three crabbed months had sour'd themselves to death / Ere I could make thee open thy white hand / And clap thyself my love" (1.2.102–104). The sole references to their affection are Hermione's playful words: "Yet, good-deed, Leontes, / I love thee not a jar o' th' clock behind / What lady she her lord" (1.2.42–44) and Leontes' declaration to the court that the defendant is "one of us too much belov'd." In several places where references to their love would seem natural, Shakespeare omits them. In the introductory scene, for instance, the picture drawn of the fortunate Leontes includes no mention of a wife. Yet, in *Pandosto*, it is largely the ideal love between Pandosto and Bellaria that makes Fortune envious, and causes her to turn her wheel, and darken "their bright sun of prosperity with the misty clouds of mishap and misery" (p. 3). Again, in the trial scene, where Hermione is listing the joys of her past life, she speaks tenderly of her children, but, of Leontes, she recalls only that she once had his "favor."

By stressing an idealized love between Othello and Desdemona, Shakespeare raises the theme of jealousy to tragic intensity: although, in sixteenth century thought, jealousy is "a weake malady of the soule, absurd, vaine, terrible and tyrannicall,"[14] it may be partially excused when it is the jealousy of a husband or wife for a dearly loved mate.[15] Benedetto Varchi explains that the highest form of jealousy springs from love—"when we estimate and prise the delight we take in the Partie we love, at so high a rate, as we would engrosse it wholly unto our selves, and when wee thinke, or imagine, it will decrease and waxe less, if it should be communicated, or lent unto another." Closely related to this love-jealousy is that "Jealousie which proceedeth from Passion, when we covet to enjoy or possesse that which we most love and like, wonderfully fearing lest we should lose possession thereof, as if our Mistresse should become a secret sweet Friend unto another man."[16] Because Othello has "garnered up his heart" in the soul and body of Desdemona, his jealousy is of these "nobler" kinds.

Jealousy which does not spring from deep love or passion, in contrast, is more selfish, more nearly related to envy and greed than to love. Varchi divides such jealousy into two kinds: "Jealousie which springeth from Propertie or Right," when we feel that we own some-one else; and closely related to this, "jealousie which cometh in respect of a man's reputation and Honour," where honor is, according to Varchi's English translator, "the reputation and credit or the good name or fame of a Man."

It is such petty, selfish jealousy that afflicts Leontes. His chief worry is that "They're here with me already; whisp'ring . . . / 'Sicilia is a so-forth!'" (1.2.217–218). His greatest torment is that he is being laughed at:

> Camillo and Polixenes
> Laugh at me, make their pastime at my sorrow.
> They should not laugh if I could reach them; nor
> Shall she, within my pow'r.   (2.3.23–26)

Othello, too, fears scorn. But his jealousy comes from a deeper source:

> But, alas, to make me
> A fixed figure for the time of scorn
> To point his slow unmoving finger at!
> Yet could I bear that too; well, very well.
> But there where I have garner'd up my heart,
> Where either I must live or bear no life,
> The fountain from the which my current runs
> Or else dries up—to be discarded thence!
>   (4.2.53–60)

For Othello, mere fear of scorn is nothing compared with the anguish of love lost.

Throughout the "tragic" section of *The Winter's Tale*, Leontes' character is in keeping with the pettiness of his passion. Robert Greene gives two specific reasons for Pandosto's nobility: "Pandosto, whose fortunate success in wars against his foes, and bountiful courtesy towards his friends in peace, made him to be greatly feared and loved of all men" (p. 2)—i.e., Pandosto, before jealousy over-took him, was a courageous warrior and a generous lord. Leontes, in contrast, is a frightened man, afraid to take open revenge on Polix-enes, who is "himself too mighty / And in his party, his alliance." He will instead revenge himself on his helpless wife. He has not even the courage of his diseased convictions; determined to put Her-mione's "bastard" child to death, he gives in to the persuasion of his courtiers that he "change this purpose," declares that he is "a feather for each wind that blows," and decides that the child shall live. He as quickly changes his mind again and has the child abandoned "to some remote and desert place"—a course more cruel and cowardly than his first plan of having it immediately killed.

Even his method of attack on Polixenes is a cowardly one. Poison-ing one's enemies "is an unfair death-trick" on the Elizabethan stage, notes Mary C. Hyde; "as a method of murder, it cannot ethical-ly claim the same respect as pure slaughter, since it assumes . . . that the victim is caught . . . wholly unprotected."[17] The murder of Polixenes would have been especially cowardly, in that the poison was "no rash potion / But a ling'ring dram that should not work / Maliciously like poison." Leontes, then, is no courageous warrior, and the "bounteous courtesy" of Pandosto is also little in evidence in the "play" we are considering. Toward the close of *The Winter's Tale*, a bountiful, courteous Leontes indeed appears. But not so in "the Leontes-story." The play opens with elaborate compliments on the magnificent entertainment Polixenes and his followers have re-ceived in Sicilia, but this gives way quickly to the single dramatization of Leontes' "bounteous courtesy": the scene of his almost too persis-tent urging of Polixenes to delay his departure.

In substituting cowardice for courage in Leontes' character, and in underplaying his generosity, Shakespeare leaves us little to admire in Leontes, for he bestows upon him no virtues to replace those he removes. One might argue that we see too little of Leontes in his normal state to be able to judge of his true character, but Shakespeare had long since developed his own technique for dealing with such situations. In the early scenes of *Antony and Cleopatra*, for instance, Antony is introduced to us as already a "strumpet's fool," but his present condition is constantly contrasted with the former Antony by references to his "goodly eyes / That o'er the files and musters of the war / Have glow'd like plated Mars"; to his "captain's heart / Which in the scuffles of great fights hath burst / The buckles on his breast" (1.1.2–8). We are not allowed to forget that Antony is "the triple pillar of the world" (1.1.12).

Willard Farnham finds that the "praise" which such heroes as Antony and Macbeth receive from other characters helps determine our feeling for such "deeply flawed" characters. "When we do admire these children of folly, we remember that though they are ridiculed in their dramas, they are also praised, and praised in no mean terms."[18] Farnham's appraisal could apply to *Othello* as well. Because Othello falls victim to Iago's trap, he is in danger of losing our respect; to prevent this, Shakespeare has other characters repeatedly remind us of the hero's greatness. We are told of his heroism and courage in battle; he is always "valiant Othello": Desdemona refers to his "honours and his valiant parts," and helps us to see Othello through her admiring eyes. Later in the play, references to his virtues become very important in helping to shape our reactions. Just after Othello's cruel public attack on Desdemona, at a moment when we have little sympathy and no admiration for the Moor, Lodovico reminds us of Othello's essential nobility:

> Is this the noble Moor whom our full Senate
> Call all in all sufficient? Is this the Nature
> Whom passion could not shake? whose solid virtue

> The shot of accident nor dart of chance
> Could neither graze nor pierce?

$$(4.1.275–279)$$

And again, after the murder of Desdemona, Lodovico reminds us of Othello's earlier virtue: "O thou Othello that wert once so good" (5.2.291). And Cassio passes the final judgment for us in his comment on Othello's suicide: "This did I fear . . . , / For he was great of heart" (5.2.360–361).

Considering Shakespeare's usual practice of commenting on the virtues of his tragic heroes through the other characters in the play, it is significant that not once in "the Leontes-story" does a character refer to Leontes' goodness, or single out any of his virtues for praise. Camillo best knows Leontes and is first to learn of his jealous madness, yet in his references to "a master . . . in rebellion with himself" there is no mention of a Leontes who was once so noble. Camillo reports to Polixenes, that he, Camillo, is appointed to murder him. Polixenes asks "By whom, Camillo?" And at Camillo's answer: "By the king," Polixenes makes no exclamation of astonishment that one so great should sink so low; he merely asks "For what?" And in his later analysis of the situation, he notes that the jealousy is for "a precious creature": "As she's rare / Must it be great; and as his person's mighty, / Must it be violent" (1.2.452–454). Yet even this remark is no comment on Leontes' greatness of soul: Polixenes is simply repeating the commonplace that men in positions of might were most violent in their jealousies.[19]

On the other hand there are numerous references to Leontes' tyranny, to his "dangerous unsafe lunes." Paulina accuses him of madness, calls his fancy "weak-hinged," and sees that his action makes him "ignoble . . . Yea, scandalous to the world" (2.3.119–120)—an echo of Antigonus's earlier "aside," in which he answers

14

the king's "We are to speak in public; for this business / Will raise us all" with the comment "To laughter, as I take it, / If the good truth were known" (2.1.197–199). Antigonus's recognition that Leontes is an essentially laughable creature shocks us out of any tragic pity we might have felt for Leontes, and reminds us that the "jealous husband" is, in fact, a stock comic character.

Leontes himself draws attention to the resemblance between his situation and that of the typical cuckolded husband:

> There have been
> (Or I am much deceiv'd) cuckolds ere now;
> And many a man there is (even at this present,
> Now, while I speak this) holds his wife by th' arm
> That little thinks she had been sluic'd in's absence
>
> .   .   .   .
>
> Nay, there's comfort in't
> Whiles other men have gates, and those gates open'd
> (As mine) against their will. Should all despair
> That have revolted wives, the tenth of mankind
> Would hang themselves. Physic for't there's none.
>
> .   .   .   .
>
> Many thousand on's
> Have the disease, and feel't not.
>
> (1.2.190–207)

This ready acceptance of his common lot with the typical cuckold is a far cry from Othello's view of his own position:

> Yet, 'tis the plague of great ones;
> Prerogativ'd are they less than the base.
> 'Tis destiny unshunnable, like death.
> Even then this forked plague is fated to us
> When we do quicken.   (3.3.273–277)

If Othello is cuckolded, then cuckoldry is the plague of great men.

Leontes seems closer to Ford, or perhaps to Kitely, than he does to Othello. Kitely, Ben Jonson's comic jealous husband in *Every Man in His Humour*, is, like Leontes, a self-deluded creature driven to all of Leontes' frenzies of jealousy. He, too, suffers from "poore mortalls plague." The jealous husband in the 1598 version of this play, that in which "Will. Shakespeare" appeared as a "principall Comoedian," was an Italian, Thorello. Whether or not Shakespeare had comic Thorello in mind when he drew the character of Leontes, the fact is that Shakespeare only sporadically raises Leontes above the level of the Kitely/Thorello figure.

He refuses, for example, to introduce into *The Winter's Tale* an Iago figure. In *Othello*, as we noted, Shakespeare raised the tragic significance of the story by retaining the villainous Ensign, by increasing the complexity of the Ensign's character, and by relating him to ubiquitous forces of evil. Now, in the story of Leontes, there is no villain—except for Leontes' own imagination. This fact has a profound effect on our feelings about Leontes. We might analyze his passion and his possible madness as extenuating circumstances, arguing that they are in the same category as "external temptations to sin,"[20] but our natural reaction is that his crimes, had they succeeded, would have been the more heinous for his self-deception.

The fact is that Leontes simply "too much believed [his] own suspicions." That Leontes' fancy was, as Paulina put it, "weak-hinged," that his imagination was so diseased as to "breed chimeres and monsters," and that his reason was so weak that the corrupt thought of a moment could compel a monomaniacal belief, indicates a basic defect in Leontes' character. According to sixteenth- and seventeenth-century writers, the healthy imagination presents only true images. George Puttenham notes that "the phantastical part of man (if it be not disordered) is a representer of the best, most comely, and beau-

tiful images . . . to the soul, and according to their very truth."[21]
Robert Burton, too (*The Anatomy of Melancholy*, pp. 220–221),
states that it is only the corrupt imagination "which prefers falsehood
before that which is right and good, deluding the soul with false
shows and suppositions." And he relates the "false and corrupt
imagination" to a general contamination in the man: "And although
this phantasy of ours be a subordinate faculty to reason, and should
be ruled by it, yet in many men, through inward or outward dis-
temperatures, defect of organs, which are unapt and hindered, or
otherwise contaminated, is likewise unapt, hindered, and hurt" (pp.
220–221). And an imagination so corrupt that it sees evil in those
nearest and best known to be virtuous is especially despicable, for its
imaginings are furthest from "the rectitude of reason," and show a
basic corruption in the character of the dreamer. Twentieth-century
psychology might put Burton's analysis in other terms, but we, too,
ask ourselves, in the presence of a self-deluded jealous husband, what
kind of pettiness, of self-hatred, must lie in the soul of one who can
thus imagine, thus display, himself as an object of scorn? As Pierre
Charron (1612) asks about the jealous husband: "For what doth
he but publish, put out of all doubt, bring into the light, sound with
a trumpet his owne shame and misery, and the dishonour of his owne
children?" (p. 95). Charron could well be describing Leontes, who
is not only the sounder of his own trumpet, but also the villainous
"putter-on" who has "abus'd" himself and "will be damned for't"
(2.1.141–142).

It is interesting here to remind ourselves of a point very easy to
overlook in *The Winter's Tale:* namely, that Leontes is a king.
Granted, he is a Sicilian king, and that fact might, for a Jacobean
audience, excuse certain comic excesses in his character. Yet the symbolic role of kingship runs too deep in the Renaissance psyche for all
of the traditional connotations of Leontes as *Rex*—as symbol of

some power larger than the personal—to simply disappear. The potential for tragedy, then, is great: the fate of a nation is at stake when its king acts foolishly. Hermione is not only an unjustly accused wife—she is the queen; Mamillius is the prince, the future hope of the nation; Perdita is the princess. Further tragic potential emerges when we see Leontes as the archetypal "sick king," whose kingdom will languish until he is healed. Yet Leontes' sickness is a "weak-hing'd fancy," his governance a sputtering tyranny, the "healer" of the sick kingdom a scolding shrew. Leontes is not tragically great in his sickness; he is pathetic, isolated, almost comic; and the combination of scorn and pity heaped on him by Hermione and Paulina help to strip the "sick king" paradigm of its tragic potential. Seen in these terms, Shakespeare's deliberate avoidance of the tragedy possibly inherent in the "Leontes story" seems especially striking.

Othello, though no king, falls as man originally fell, under the force of external, persuasive evil. His tragedy is no simple allegory of the fall of man, but the fact that Othello's will was overborne by Iago's machinations raises him in our minds; even man at his highest, unfallen man, chose evil at Satan's instigation. This quality of Othello's story lifts it above the more typical, but less tragic, story of Leontes. For Othello represents "man at his highest" in a way that Leontes cannot.

Primarily because of the distortion in the character of Leontes, "the Leontes-story" does not carry tragic significance. Tillyard sees the character of the tragic hero as of primary importance for tragic effect; as we have seen, Leontes, especially in this "destructive phase" of *The Winter's Tale*, is not tragically great. As for Tillyard's other requirements for tragedy, let us remember that he specified that it is through suffering that the tragic hero is somehow renewed and reconciled. Yet Leontes' suffering—in "the Leontes-story"—comes across as a shallow thing. After his son's death, Leontes' first concern is to make everything all right again. He'll "new woo the queen," "recall Camillo." Even his wife's death brings forth only: "I have deserved all tongues to talk their bitterest." Never—until we see the penitent Leontes of act 5—does he express such feeling as in Othello's self-castigating "O fool, fool, fool!" And because Leontes, in "the Leontes-story," changes so quickly from initial stateliness to mania and then to sudden repentance and an attempt to regain his former image, we cannot really suffer with him. The pity we feel is for Hermione; and sympathy for such total, abused innocence is not the "pity" proper to tragedy.[22]

As for Professor Tillyard's "conflict," his "summons to resist certain things in the universal scheme": in "the Leontes-story," there is no true conflict. Since Leontes' reason succumbs so quickly to his diseased imagination, there is little internal conflict. There is no villain for external battle, nor any "good" man strong enough to combat Leontes' tyranny. Leontes' verbal conflicts with Hermione and Paulina are not tragic encounters; indeed, they smack strongly of the comic "battle of the sexes." As in much good comedy, these females get the best of Leontes in the battles, reducing him to a querulous "Shall I be heard?" or to a ranting "A callat of boundless tongue, who / Late hath beat her husband and now baits me!" Yet Leontes is the king, and defeats the two women through his power. Even the trial is no true conflict, for a mad Leontes is both prosecutor and judge.

The battle of the sexes is not the only comic device used in this section of the play. Each of the "grave tragic personages," as G. G. Gervinus calls them,[23] is but a warped version of a stock comic character. Leontes we have seen as the "jealous husband." Hermione is more patient than Griselda; Paulina is the counterpart of Griselda's foil, Gwenthyan; and Camillo is, of course, the intriguing servant of New Comedy, as well as the bribed, defecting "murderer" of the then-popular *Jacke Drum's Entertainment* (1601). There is even a variation of the cat-and-mouse device used in *Much Ado about Nothing:* the constant false preparation of the audience for action that leads to nothing; the leading on of the audience to expect one thing, only to thwart their expectations or spring some new surprise. Dramaturgy in which the unexpected is an inherent feature can hardly foster the inevitability of tragedy.

To summarize, then, "the Leontes-story" presents a potentially tragic plot, along with many tragic accoutrements: noble figures, intense passions, deaths. But the hero of the action is so distorted away from greatness and nobility that audience identification with him repeatedly breaks down, and audience participation in his suffering occurs only occasionally. And the undermining of the "tragic world" of Sicilia with comic distortions and exaggerations gives us a world uninformed by tragic universality, one which produces an effect approaching the grotesque—that "intermingling of the laughable and the frightening which precludes the more conventional, more unequivocal sort of response that we associate with comedy or tragedy."[24]

From my analysis of "the Leontes-story," I would claim, then, that Shakespeare, in this play—and this play is Tillyard's strongest piece of evidence—was not attempting to "expand" his earlier tragedies. The last plays may, of course, be expansions of Shakespeare's tragic *vision:* Shakespeare may have come to see that tragic and comic perspectives eventually meet and that the final end of tragic separation is reunion. My own feeling is that he had long known this: both *A Midsummer Night's Dream* and the frame story of *Comedy of Errors* show considerable awareness of the interrelatedness of comic and tragic perspectives. But even if the late plays do mirror an "expanded tragic vision," as artistic expressions of that vision they show a distinct change from the mature tragedies. And to fail to recognize that change can easily lead one into searching for excellencies and profundities which do not exist in the Romances, and, more seriously, into overlooking the excellencies and profundities which indeed are there.

A similar argument holds for the alternate claim that the plays are extensions of Shakespeare's *comic* form. This claim, like Tillyard's, is an attractive one. It reminds us that comic elements indeed appear in each of the Romances; it finds support in the argument that the crucial moment in each play, thematically and structurally, is the moment of "comic recognition";[25] and it leads us to an interesting comic interpretation of "the Leontes-story": namely, that the point of this drama is to show us that man, even at his most powerful and in his moments of deepest anguish, is not as important as he thinks he is, nor should he be taken very seriously. Looking down on noble characters and tragic actions from the Olympian height of the genial Comic Spirit, we realize that even kings are rather ridiculous, that Nature is not deliberately cruel—bears "are never curst but when they are hungry" (*The Winter's Tale*, 3.3.135)—and that, with time, the most painful tragedy becomes a tale of sprites and goblins to while away a winter evening.

Yet comedy is so protean a genre that any play with a nontragic ending can, with some justification, be included in its province. In what sense is it meaningful to label the Romances "expanded Shakespearian comedy"? Expanded comic *vision*, perhaps. Undoubtedly comic vision eventually touches the tragic; undoubtedly one could claim that Shakespeare's comic vision in his last years broadened to include human evil and death within its genial gaze. Yet even if the last plays do represent Shakespeare's mature (or "sublime," or

"final") comic vision,[26] as dramatic constructs they are (when compared with Shakespearean comedy) as carefully noncomic as they
are nontragic.

We can see this if we briefly examine Shakespeare's method of
handling the "slandered maiden" fable in comic form.[27] In *Othello*
he sublimates this fable in high tragedy; in *The Winter's Tale* he
distorts the hero away from tragic greatness and refuses to breathe
into the tale those elements which would make it universally tragic.
In *Much Ado about Nothing*—a comic rendering of essentially the
same fable—he so shapes the story that its pathos will not destroy
the comic fabric. His goals in *Much Ado about Nothing* seem two-
fold: first, to protect the audience from emotional involvement in the
suffering, and, second, to provide a comic world—a world that is
essentially mirth-provoking, to borrow a few words from Samuel
Johnson's definition of comedy.[28]

To shield the audience, Shakespeare transforms the sources and
analogues of the Hero-Claudio story. He so underplays the love-
relationship that it is presented in frankly businesslike terms: Claudio, instead of being jealous, seems primarily angry at having
"rotten goods" foisted off on him. In this and other ways, Claudio
is rendered so unsympathetic a hero that critics repeatedly declare
him insufferable; and the cardboard villain, whom Shakespeare sub-
stitutes for the more usual jealous friend, is more ludicrous than
terrifying in his plain-dealing villainy.

These changes in the source-story are, to be sure, often considered
flaws in Shakespeare's handling of the story, examples of "the
evident neglect and carelessness of Shakespeare's treatment of this
part of the play." Shakespeare's "transformation of the lofty-minded
Timbreo of Bandello's novel into the rather insignificant, superficial,
uncertain Claudio" is called "absolutely repulsive"; the underplaying
of the love-relationship is viewed as an oversight on Shakespeare's

part, and Bulthaupt asks plaintively "if it would not have been possible to make Claudio's love . . . noble and profound?" Don John's lack of adequate motive is sharply criticized: in most of the analogues, the villain is in love with the heroine and wants her for himself. In many, he is the hero's best friend. Had Shakespeare retained those elements of the original stories, he could, so critics say, have involved us much more closely in the Hero–Don John–Claudio triangle.[29] Arthur Quiller-Couch criticizes Shakespeare for not presenting the scene in which the hero sees his "rival" climbing to his betrothed's window. "Such a scene," he notes, "is found in all the analogues," and, by omitting it, Shakespeare "weakens our sympathy with Claudio. . . . We cannot put ourselves in his place, deprived as we have been of the visual evidence that convinced him."[30]

Yet it seems clear that, rather than blundering, Shakespeare carefully shaped the Claudio-Hero story so that audience emotions would not be too heavily assaulted.[31] Were Claudio presented as the suffering and self-sacrificing young lover of the sources, were he and Don John close friends torn apart by their love for Hero, were we given the window scene instead of the "watch scene" which so delightfully replaces it, the Hero-Claudio story would shift so far toward the pathetic and the painful that the comic fabric of the play would be rent.

Shakespeare's methods of shielding the audience from involvement in the suffering in *Much Ado about Nothing* should be familiar to us: they are much like the distancing devices used in *The Winter's Tale*, but in *Much Ado about Nothing* the methods are used consistently and systematically. The difference here, then, is largely a matter of the degree of audience involvement. If we compare the worlds which contain the fable in *Much Ado about Nothing* and *The Winter's Tale*, however, the difference is no longer a matter of degree. The world of "the Leontes-story" is in no sense mirth-provoking, and even the world of the Bohemia section of *The Winter's Tale*—"the culmination of Shakespeare's romantic comedy," according to Norman Rabkin (p. 220)—is a world at which, when we laugh, we laugh in spite of our awareness that treachery, tortures, and hungry bears are a very real part of the fairy-tale landscape. In *Much Ado about Nothing*, in contrast, the "slandered maiden" fable is surrounded by Shakespeare's most exquisite comedy. Shakespeare places the tale of slander and deceit in the center of the comic, bustling world of Messina, and he carefully interweaves the melodrama with the Beatrice-Benedick story and the Dogberry episodes—with comedy, that is, of extraordinary quality.

Shakespeare's technique for ensuring the final comic effect of *Much Ado about Nothing* is not duplicated in his other mature comedies. In *As You Like It* and *Twelfth Night*, instead of distancing the audience from real suffering, he removes from the stories most of the elements which would tend to cause pain; instead of interweaving melodrama with high comedy, he has high comedy reign throughout. In spite of these differences in technique, I would suggest that, just as the great Shakespearean tragedies have in common, first, a hero who demands audience identification and participation in his suffering, and, second, a universally significant tragic world, so Shakespeare's mature comedies are alike in their protection of the audience from painful elements in the stories, and in their emphasis on the representation of human life as essentially mirth-provoking.

In the last plays, on the other hand, the audience is neither closely involved with the suffering of the hero (as in tragedy) nor consistently shielded from such suffering (as in comedy). Tragedy and comedy so blend in these plays that, as R. J. Kaufmann has expressed it, "our immediate participation in the suffering is not so much prevented, as it is in pure comedy, but disciplined and calculatedly occasional."[32] Again, while the world of the last plays is not informed by any universal tragic meaning, neither does it present a comic view of life: Mamillius does die of grief, and Antigonus dies in anguish even though his being eaten alive is comically described.

The blending of tragedy and comedy to create sporadic audience engagement can be found in all of the Romances, but for the moment let us return briefly to *The Winter's Tale* for one or two examples. First, in "the Leontes-story," against a somber though nontragic background, real suffering is presented for our occasional sympathy, as we are suddenly brought into the passionate, warped, and incoherent mind of the hero through his soliloquies, only to be forced into a sudden attitude of detachment when a comic spotlight is turned on him. For instance, in act 2, scene 3, Leontes enters, a near-tragic Macbeth-like figure, soliloquizing: "Nor night nor day no rest! It is but weakness / To bear the matter thus—mere weakness" (2.3.1–2). This somber, formal mood is sustained for many lines. Leontes then sees Paulina with the baby, and immediately becomes a pathetic, near-comic figure (a posture he maintains until the end of this long scene). With his comic outburst:

> Away with that audacious lady! Antigonus,
> I charg'd thee that she should not come about me.
> I knew she would. (2.3.42–44)

—an outburst which reveals his dread of the scolding but powerless female—we cannot possibly continue to suffer with him as with a tragic hero.

In the Bohemia section of *The Winter's Tale*, the method of "the Leontes-story" is reversed; instead of comic devices undercutting tragic emotions, we find the painful invading the comic world. Into the realm of fairy-tale princesses, shepherds, and true love come the rage of a suddenly cruel Polixenes and the treachery of a seemingly helpful Camillo,[33] who seems a "preserver" to Florizel, who furnishes letters and secret advice to "save" the young couple, but who, as he tells us in an aside, frames the entire business to serve his own ends, and gives no thought to the fate of the young couple as he announces to the audience, "What I do next shall be to tell the King / Of this escape and whither they are bound" (4.4.676ff).

The grotesque world of the Romances—that world created by the blending of the comic and the horrible—can be illustrated easily in scenes from each of the Romances. One thinks immediately of the transition scene in *The Winter's Tale*, with its ghost vision, its pathetic babe, its humorous rustics, its soaring, mocking sea, and, of course, Antigonus's bear.[34] Or one thinks of the scene in *Cymbeline* in which Imogen awakes from deathlike sleep to find beside her a headless corpse which she thinks is that of her husband, but whom we know to be the lout Cloten, killed before he succeeded in finding and raping her. Her anguish arias of grief, her positive limb-by-limb identification of the body as that of the paragon, Posthumus, create a moment at once as ludicrous as the Titania-Bottom scenes and as moving as the most effective Shakespearean tragedy.[35] *The Tempest* gives us the laughable and the horrible combined in the figure of the beast-man Caliban who lusts after Miranda and who urges his new gods to revenge him on the sleeping Prospero: "brain him, / . . . or with a log / Batter his skull, or paunch him with a stake, / Or cut his wesand with thy knife." *The Tempest* also gives us muted grotesque moments in such scenes as that which introduces the Court Party on the island, where the scornful villains, Antonio and Sebastian, succeed, as Coleridge noted, in "making the good ridiculous" as they echo every word of Gonzalo with derisive puns and jibes.[36]

To call these plays "expanded tragedy" or "expanded comedy," then, is to overlook the very careful blending of tragic and comic effects in the plays and to encourage that distortion of tone which so often plagues criticism of the Romances.[37] "Calculatedly occasional" involvement of the audience with the suffering; a nontragic, non-comic world containing both the laughable and the frightening, the sublime and the ridiculous: these are characteristics of the last plays which distinguish them from Shakespearean comedy and Shakespearean tragedy, and which, I feel, link them into a common Shakespearean "kind"—a variety of tragicomedy, but differing from tragicomedy as it is normally defined. The Romances are unlike those more typical tragicomedies (or *drames*) which avoid the extremes of comic or tragic emotions, holding "life's incongruities . . . in ironic perspective" (Cyrus Hoy, p. 8). Instead, these late Shakespearean tragicomedies focus on tragedy as it verges on the ludicrously overstated, on comedy as it reaches out to involve the tragically painful. They expand the implications of tragic and comic perspectives, juxtapose tragic and comic effects, include death and weddings, throw open the world to gods, spirits, beasts, and monsters, and force the spectator to oscillate between (or to experience simultaneously) sentimentally naive responses and a sophisticated awareness of the ironic.

Shakespeare's methods of so blending comic and tragic devices and perspectives are different in each of the three Romances. In *Cymbeline*, instead of *The Winter's Tale*'s surface tragic/comic split, the basic shape of the play tends toward the tragic, and many of the play's motifs are reminiscent of Shakespeare's tragedies: blindly stupid fathers, Iago-like villains, violently jealous lovers, marching armies, prophecies, war—but here the motifs are parodied in the telling, and the tragically-tending story takes a sudden last-scene swing away from multiple deaths to deathbed repentances, recognitions by token, and lyric reunions. In *Cymbeline*, as in "the Leontes-story," the suffering is real, and the audience is distanced from the hero through comic effects. But here the technique is somewhat more complex than in *The Winter's Tale*, for we are made to view Posthumus and his problems as simultaneously tragic and ridiculous. Post-humus's diatribe against women, for instance, based on his mistaken belief in Imogen's infidelity, resounds at one moment with the despair of a Hamlet or the anguish of an Othello, and at the next sounds like a comic parody of both. When he reaches the lines: "I'll write against them / Detest them, curse them," we feel almost certain that this is comedy (the lines are near echoes of Claudio's speech in *Much Ado about Nothing*, 4.1.57); but most of the speech, as Bertrand Evans notes, "surpasses the finest work Shakespeare had done with scenes that demand simultaneous, mutually contradictory responses."[38]

In *Cymbeline*, as in "the Leontes-story," Shakespeare uses a fable which had twice appeared in his earlier work. One of the central fables in *Cymbeline* is the fable of the "exiled daughter," treated tragically in *King Lear* and comically in *As You Like It*. In *Cymbeline*, as in *King Lear*, a daughter is driven into exile by her father's blind stupidity; as in *As You Like It*, the exiled daughter goes wandering in the woods disguised as a boy, and, in the end, finds both her father and her true love. But, in *Cymbeline*, the audience is sometimes involved in the very real suffering of the characters, sometimes detached from this suffering by the comic excesses of the leading characters; and, as in *The Winter's Tale*, the grotesque world in which the heroine finds herself is never tragically significant nor truly mirth-provoking.

In *The Tempest*, we again get sporadic involvement and a non-tragic, noncomic world. But in this play the suffering itself is "distanced"—by time (much of the suffering had occurred twelve years earlier and is merely described in the play), by Prospero's superiority to ordinary mortals, and by comic treatment of suffering itself. Caliban's anguish in the grip of "cramps and pinches" is at once pathetic and ludicrous; the abortive attempt on the life of Prospero has poi-

gnant elements, in that it recalls the usurpation of Prospero's dukedom and dramatizes his failure to civilize Caliban: yet it is portrayed
as ludicrously comic, and is halted by a grotesque hunt with Prospero
and Ariel "setting on" spirit dogs.

The basic shape of *The Tempest* is that of comedy: Bernard Knox
has compared the action and characters of the play to those of Roman
new comedy, and his argument is quite convincing.[39] But in this play,
too, tragic and comic motifs blend bewilderingly. From the tragedies
come the storm, the threatened deaths by murder or drowning, the
griefs and dirges; from the comedies come the young love motifs:
love at first sight, trials suffered for love, marriage celebrations. The
blending of tragic and comic elements creates an effect sometimes
disturbing (as in the scene in which Gonzalo's political speech is
ridiculed), sometimes grotesque, and sometimes tolerantly ironic
("O brave new world / That has such Creatures in't." " 'Tis new to
thee.").

Shakespeare's care in creating, in *The Tempest*, a play that (like
Cymbeline and *The Winter's Tale*) stands carefully poised beyond
tragedy or comedy, though linked to both forms, can best be under-
stood if we think briefly of his earlier handling of the basic *Tempest*
fable—the fable of the "usurping brother"—as comedy (in *As You
Like It*) and as tragedy (in *Hamlet*). The plot situations of the three
plays—with the exiled (or murdered) rulers, the conflict between
brothers, and the emphasis on the father-child relationship—have
much in common. Yet, in terms of the tragic and comic matrices
suggested earlier, *Hamlet* provides us with a hero who demands
almost complete audience identification in a world which, though
occasionally leavened by high wit or coarse humor, essentially em-
bodies the tragic vision of a noble human being suffering and dying
in conflict with his universe, while *As You Like It* gives us, in Duke
Senior and Rosalind, major characters who do not demand identifica-

tion (we never enter deeply into their minds), but with whom we may identify without losing our comic perspective, since Shakespeare has abstracted from their situations all elements of pain. Theirs is a genial world in which evil melts away or is suddenly converted to good.

In *The Tempest*, we find ourselves poised between these two earlier treatments of the fable. Prospero's situation is externally like Duke Senior's, except that, instead of being surrounded by a band of jolly courtiers, he is alone on an island with two servants—a spirit and a monster—and his daughter. Like the ghost in *Hamlet*, his consuming wish is to remove his usurping brother from the throne. He has struggled for twelve years to perfect his magic powers: first, in order to survive, then in order to return to his dukedom and marry his daughter to the prince. With a few well-chosen soliloquies to bring us into the mind of a suffering, lonely, but courageous Prospero, Shakespeare could have given us in *The Tempest* the "expanded tragedy" that Tillyard envisaged. There is certainly evil enough on Prospero's island to have led to tragedy. And Shakespeare could have made Prospero's struggles against his desire to revenge himself on his enemies, or Prospero's grief at the loss of his beloved Miranda to Ferdinand, into the compelling stuff of deeply moving tragic drama. But if such struggles, such griefs, such thoughts move Prospero, we do not share them. In a sense we see the action from the point of view of the all-powerful Prospero, and we accept the fact that he is wise, usually benevolent, and justified in dealing with his enemies as he chooses. But we do not really "know" Prospero; more specifically, we do not suffer with him. When he becomes deeply angered at the thought of Caliban's rebellion, we are as surprised as is Miranda. And when he answers Ariel's plea that he show mercy to his victims with the announcement that he will do so, we may argue about whether he is here converted from vengeance to mercy, or whether he had intended mercy all along, but we never really know what had been in his mind or heart.

The Tempest, then, gives us a hero with whom we tend to identify, but with whom we do not suffer. We know that he has suffered; we sense the gloom and anger that still move him. But we are never brought closely enough in contact with his feelings to enable us to suffer with him. Miranda, too, has an intermediate position. She is no comic heroine at whom we laugh, or with whom we may enjoy the foibles of the world. Life, to her, is serious and wonderful, and her naiveté is part of her charm, not something at which we scoff. Yet she is surely no tragic heroine. Between her and the evils of her world—represented primarily by Caliban's lust—stands the all-powerful Prospero. As for the world of *The Tempest:* elements of humor and of horror there are in plenty, especially in the Caliban and Court Party scenes. Evil and discord exist, but because all is under Prospero's beneficent, powerful, all-seeing control, the world is in no way tragic. Yet—again because of the pervasive spirit of Prospero—the vision of the play is not comic. To Prospero, life is a serious matter, in no sense mirth-provoking. Prospero's world is one which will inevitably crush the weak, exile or kill the unwary, violate the innocent, make fools of the good—unless a superior superhuman force intervenes, imprisoning the bestial in rocks and placing within a charmed circle the more civilized forces of evil.[40]

In each of the last plays, then—each characterized by sporadic, carefully controlled audience engagement and by a world simultaneously frightening, awesome, grotesque, and lyrically beautiful—there is a disturbing blend of tragic and comic forms, elements, and motifs. The plays do grow out of Shakespeare's major tragedies and comedies: the similarity of fables, incidents, characters, and devices tie the Romances firmly to Shakespeare's work in the two major genres.[41] Yet they are a kind in themselves—intricate, playful, disturbing mixtures, perhaps best seen as Romance variants of the tragicomic mode. As in the Greek Romances which underlie them,[42] the tragicomic blend allows the playwright to escape the bounds of either tragedy or comedy—tragedy which takes man and his illusions seriously, and comedy which so lightly dismisses or punctures such illusions in the service of common sense and reason. As in Greek Romance, "tragic" events take place in a cruel world: babies are abandoned, wives unjustly accused, murders and rapes attempted, loves destroyed. Yet the comic form prevails: seas prove kind, Time heals as well as destroys, statues come to life and are warm.

According to Herbert McArthur, the comic spirit, which comes not to destroy value systems but to correct their imbalances, "cannot survive defeat. Only tragedy dares to suggest that something can be left when everything is gone, to assert life in the midst of death and happiness in the midst of suffering."[43] Yet Greek Romances, and Shakespeare's last plays, allow comedy to survive defeat; and their authors make us believe their happy endings by so blending comedy and tragedy that, throughout, we question the seriousness of all the events, question the reality of all the appearances. Leontes is tragically jealous, and he does terrible things—but he can repent, can live with the consequences of his actions, and can be reunited with his wife and daughter (all with our consent) because none of it is quite real. Because of the comic distortions in the "tragic phase" of his story, the terrible events—Leontes' madness, Hermione's trial, the abandonment of Perdita—are not for us devastating; they can, as we watch, fade into the past and become part of the series of strange events which make up this old tale.

One is reminded of Morton Bloomfield's perceptive comments on the blending of tragedy and comedy in another great romance, "Sir Gawain and the Green Knight": "The great charm of the poem perhaps is due to this curious mystery which both amuses and sobers, delights and frightens us at the same time, as it teeters on the edge of tragedy and defeat but at last brings us back to the solid ground of a happy ending."[44] Bloomfield suggests that the long-ago-and-far-away atmosphere helps to hold the tragic at bay (it is, he says, "slightly comic just because it is the past"), but he also notes that the author deliberately keeps a distance between the poem and the reader: "If the reader were to get too closely involved, he might find a tragic horror too great to be borne. The wonder would turn to fear and the delight and curiosity which are always a product of objectivity would be lost" (p. 18). So, too, with the *Aethiopica*, and with *The Winter's Tale*, *Cymbeline*, and *The Tempest*. As tragedy and comedy blend, we take man and his very real suffering seriously while simultaneously recognizing the folly of it all—in the play and in our lives. Seen from within, and in the present, the events of our lives are to us significant, sometimes overwhelming, sometimes terrifying; yet distance them by time, by a sudden vision of how they appear to another or how they look in a larger context, and they seem suddenly trivial, perhaps a bit comic. Shakespearean tragedy takes us into the individual experience, gives us entrance into the mind and emotions of a Hamlet or a Lear, reveals to us a world of truly tragic import in which heroic man and his acts are significant; Shakespearean comedy lifts us out of the experience by showing us the wonderful follies of the human species—the comic mistakes (in language, in mistaken identities), the infatuations, the silliness of the man who takes himself or his world too seriously. Each view is in its way true; by juxtaposing the two incompatible views in the Romances, Shakespeare validates and invalidates both views and enables us, if we will, to gain a marvelous double perspective on life.

"Doleful matter merrily set down" delights us, surprises us, and teaches us that man is a giddy thing set in an unfathomable universe and that we, like Leontes, live in a world both tragic and comic: that our lives are simultaneously actions that we go on for our better grace and tales for a winter evening, full of sprites and goblins.

"A Very Pleasant Thing Indeed, and Sung Lamentably": Dramatic Tactics in the Romances

In his last phase, when hardly bothering
To be a dramatist, the Master turned away
From his taut plots and complex characters
To tapestried romances.
            —Louis MacNeice, "Autolycus"[1]

In the Romances, Shakespeare not only blends tragedy and comedy, but he also yokes divergent theatrical styles, with the result that the dramatic technique of the plays has come under severe critical attack. Until recently the attitude held firm that MacNeice was right: that, indeed, Shakespeare "hardly bothered to be a dramatist" when writing his last plays.[2] Since the 1960s the critical tide has been turning; much that was previously called "primitive" or "crude" is now called "artificial" or "theatrical"[3]—yet, in spite of this shift in critical perspective the dramatic technique in these plays is still largely misunderstood.

The misunderstandings and confusions arise in large part from the failure of critics to recognize the complexity and deliberateness of the tactical dramaturgy of the Romances. Dramatic tactics—"the art of getting . . . characters on and off the stage, of conveying information to the audience, and so forth"[4]—are the mechanics of stagecraft, conventions which change from one dramatic period to another, as stage-audience relationships change and as that which is "natural" in one period becomes "artificial" or "crude" in another. Since conven-

35

tions change, a dramatist must be keenly sensitive to the accepted tactics of his time. Given that sensitivity, however, the dramatist may then choose how he wishes to use dramatic tactics. In general he chooses to make them as inconspicuous as possible: when audience attention is called to the mechanics of getting characters on and off stage, or when an audience is made aware that a speech is not a necessary part of the ongoing action, but has been inserted for the benefit of audience information, the illusion that the stage action is somehow "real" is broken. Dramatists who create "representational" drama (drama which is "based on creating the illusion that it represents a world entirely different from that in which the audience is while in the theatre"[5]) avoid obtrusive tactics and weave entrances and exits and exposition into the fabric of the play. On the other hand dramatists who wish to call our attention to the theatrical medium, who create "presentational" dramas in which the thrust is toward the "presenting" of a stage world rather than the "representing" of an illusively "real" world, frequently use for their own purposes the illusion-breaking properties of obtrusive tactics, and add such tactics to their repertoire of presentational devices. In Shakespeare's Romances, presentational and representational styles exist side by side, and a complex tactical dramaturgy is the result.

Shakespeare's interest in presentational devices which affect audience detachment—dialogue which comments on the fictiveness of the play world, spectacle, highly stylized language—has long been recognized.[6] His fascination with audience response is, in fact, so great that his plays provide uncanny documentation for Edward Bullough's theory of aesthetic distancing.[7] For example, Claudius, in "The Mousetrap" scene, is the "underdistanced" audience: because he is touched too nearly by Hamlet's play, he becomes personally frightened and threatened, and must rush from the "theater" demanding light. In contrast, Theseus and Hippolyta are the "overdistanced" audience: the clumsy acting, bad writing, and obtrusive tactics of "Pyramus and Thisbe" destroy for them any possible dramatic illusion, and they are merely amused and annoyed by a story inherently poignant.

Knowing of Shakespeare's preoccupation with the stage-audience relationship, we need to observe with great care his use of dramatic tactics in the late plays. If we do not observe carefully, we either become insensitive to the impact of the tactics (and other presentational devices) as Shakespeare employs them in these plays, or we note the strange disturbances and dislocations of dramatic style, and either overemphasize the artifice in the Romances, or else find it all too easy to agree with those who bemoan the "flaws" in the plays and regret that plays which are so profound in insight are so badly constructed.[8] If, however, we do proceed carefully, if we assume that, even in *Cymbeline*, Shakespeare knew exactly what he was doing and that the strange tactics are a part of the larger plan of the play, we find on examining the tactical dramaturgy that we are led into important insights about the Romances.

Since *Cymbeline* has been the Romance most often attacked for its tactical flaws,[9] let us begin our examination of tactical dramaturgy with this play, taking as our sample *Cymbeline* 1.5. In this short scene (eighty-seven lines) Shakespeare has considerable information to impart to the audience, and several entrances and exits to effect, and the tactics of the scene are amusingly obtrusive. The scene opens at the king's court in Britain, where Imogen has been left a virtual prisoner after the banishment of her husband Posthumus. Onstage come the wicked stepmother-queen, a retinue of ladies, and the queen's doctor, Cornelius.

> QUEEN: Whiles yet the dew's on ground, gather those flowers.
> Make haste. Who has the note of them?

LADY: I, madam.
QUEEN: Dispatch.   *Exeunt Ladies.*
                                                          (1.5.1–3)

Having thus brusquely cleared the stage of unwanted listeners, the
queen turns to the doctor, and to the real business of the scene:

> QUEEN: Now, Master Doctor, have you brought those drugs?
>   (l. 4)

Cornelius hands her the drugs with expressed misgivings. The box
he hands her contains, he says,

> most poisonous compounds,
> Which are the movers of a languishing death,
> But though slow, deadly.   (Ll. 8–10)

Twenty lines of dialogue between the queen and the doctor (ll.
5–25) center on these "deadly poisons": the queen says that she
wants to do experiments on animals; the doctor warns her against
hardening her heart with such experiments. We learn later that the
dialogue is pointless: the doctor is lying about the nature of the
drugs, and the queen is lying about her intentions. Her real aims are
revealed in an "aside" which serves as entrance announcement for
Pisanio (Imogen's friend and Posthumus's servant):

> QUEEN [aside]: Here comes a flattering rascal. Upon him
>   Will I first work. He's for his master,
>   And enemy to my son.   (Ll. 27–29)

The queen then dismisses the doctor with a standard, if brusque,
exit request:

> Doctor, your service for this time is ended;
> Take your own way.   (Ll. 30–31)

The doctor then utters his own "aside":

> I do suspect you, madam;
> But you shall do no harm. (Ll. 31–32)

The queen takes Pisanio away from center stage with a "stand aside" request:

> QUEEN [to Pisanio]: Hark thee, a word.

leaving the doctor free to move forward and explain everything to the audience:

> CORNELIUS [aside]: I do not like her. She doth think she has
> Strange ling'ring poisons. I do know her spirit
> And will not trust one of her malice with
> A drug of such damn'd nature. Those she has
> Will stupefy and dull the sense awhile;
> Which first, perchance, she'll prove on cats and dogs,
> Then afterward up higher; but there is
> No danger in what show of death it makes,
> More than the locking up the spirits a time,
> To be more fresh, reviving. She is fool'd
> With a most false effect; and I the truer
> So to be false with her. (Ll. 33–44)

Thus does Cornelius, in Muriel Bradbrook's words, "dispose summarily of the old convention of a sleeping potion which appears to be a poison." To Miss Bradbrook, this soliloquy (technically an "aside") is "one of the most amusingly naive in Shakespeare"; it was attacked by Samuel Johnson on the grounds that "the speaker is under no strong pressure of thought; he is neither resolving, repenting, suspecting, nor deliberating, and yet makes a long speech, to tell himself what himself knows." Cornelius is, of course, telling the audience, not himself—and the speech is a necessary one: when it is omitted, Imogen's later apparent death and resurrection make no sense.[10]

As Cornelius finishes his "aside," the queen once again dismisses him from the stage:

> QUEEN: No further service, Doctor,
>   Until I send for thee.
> CORNELIUS: I humbly take my leave.
>   *Exit*
>   (Ll. 44–45)

Then she and Pisanio move forward to continue a conversation begun in pantomime during Cornelius's address:

> QUEEN: Weeps she still, say'st thou? Dost thou think in time
>   She will not quench and let instructions enter
>   Where folly now possesses? Do thou work.
>   When thou shalt bring me word she loves my son,
>   I'll tell thee on the instant thou art then
>   As great as is thy master.   (Ll. 46–51)

The queen continues (ll. 51–75) in the face of Pisanio's unbroken silence, to urge him with bribes, threats, and cajolery to turn against Posthumus. Since, however, she transfers the drugs to him early in the monologue (l. 60) under the impression that she has handed him "deadly poisons," she obviously has no hope of making him her ally. The long ornate speech is no more than a cover for the transfer of the drugs, as she herself makes clear in soliloquy:

> QUEEN: A sly and constant knave,
>   Not to be shak'd; the agent for his master,

And the remembrancer of her to hold
The handfast to her lord. I have given him that
Which, if he take, shall quite unpeople her
Of leigers for her sweet, and which she after,
Except she bend her humour, shall be assur'd
To taste of too.   (Ll. 75–82)

This soliloquy, which outlines for us the queen's wicked scheme to get rid first of Pisanio, then of Imogen, is, on the surface, a conventional self-descriptive monologue—one, that is, in which the villain openly describes his evil plans.[11] Since we know that the box contains, not poison, but a sleeping potion, we do not feel the normal anxiety that such a speech should arouse. On the other hand, since Pisanio has been told that the box contains "precious medicines"—a token of the queen's further favors to him—we do feel a rather bemused curiosity about what will come of it all.

At this point Pisanio returns with the retinue of ladies who are thus greeted by the queen:

So, so. Well done, well done.
The violets, cowslips, and the primeroses
Bear to my closet. Fare thee well, Pisanio.
Think on my words.
                    Exeunt Queen and Ladies

To which Pisanio, alone onstage, replies:

And shall do.
But when to my good lord I prove untrue,
I'll choke myself. There's all I'll do for you!
                              Exit

(Ll. 85–87)

This closing couplet of Pisanio's drew from H. H. Furness an incredulous: "Did William Shakespeare write this doggerel?" (to which J. Nosworthy replied, "The probable answer is 'Alas, yes!' ").[12]

It is no wonder that the tactics of scenes such as this should for so long have been seen as "crude" or "primitive"—that is, as throwbacks to an earlier theater: the asides and soliloquies are explicitly didactic and audience-directed, and the exits and entrances handled in a manner reminiscent of much earlier drama. In order to understand why Shakespeare chose on occasion to use such tactics in his Romances we need to take a brief look at the use of presentational tactics in earlier drama, and a more extensive look at the history of Shakespeare's own use of such tactics.

In medieval drama presentational tactics are dominant.[13] Information is often conveyed to the audience through direct "telling" rather than indirect "showing" or "revealing"; entrances and exits are noted and explained. Muriel Bradbrook points out that the personages in medieval drama "convey information directly to the audience, not only of their circumstances—

> 'I am a lord that michle is of might,
> Prince of all Jewry, Sir Pilate I hight'
> (Wakefield Miracle Play of the Crucifixion)

—but of their feelings, motives and intentions. Nothing was obliquely stated or left to be inferred by the audience" (*Elizabethan Stage Conditions*, p. 87). As William McCollom reminds us, the influence of the presentational aspects of medieval drama was felt long after the beginning of the Renaissance.[14] "Presentational" style prevails, for example, in Shakespeare's earliest dramas, where there is the inclination to "tell" the story rather than to dramatize it and the tendency to recognize openly the presence of the audience. We may, if we like, assume that such tactics were accepted at this time as the natural, "realistic" ways to present a story on stage; the fact that most of Shakespeare's early plays use other devices which seem to us deliberately theatrical (formal patternings, set speeches, etc.), would encourage this belief. On the other hand, we may assume with William McCollom that the audience in the mid-1590s would have sensed a growth from a "more theatrical" to a "more realistic" style of drama as Shakespeare moved from *The Comedy of Errors* to, say, *1 Henry IV*. In any case, it is clear, as we shall see in the following pages, that Shakespeare's use of inherited, presentational conventions changed drastically during his writing career. In his early plays, as we shall see, Shakespeare employs expository soliloquies and asides, entrance signals and exit announcements, simply as presentational elements in essentially presentational dramas. As his general style shifts toward the representational, there is a corresponding change in his use of tactical conventions. Soliloquies become introspective; expository soliloquies, when he uses them, serve their purpose quickly and then pull the audience back into the play through illusive language or else move quickly into dialogue or action. Asides almost disappear, and entrance announcements and exit requests become a part of realistic dialogue. Shakespeare's sudden departure in *Cymbeline* from the path he had been following of fewer and fewer soliloquies and asides to the burgeoning wealth of four hundred thirty lines of soliloquy (*Coriolanus*, written shortly before *Cymbeline*, has only thirty-six)[15] is remarkable. This revival of the soliloquy, and the return in this play to obtrusive entrance announcements and doggerel exit signals seem to point to a renewed interest in presentational tactics—tactics which can be joined with other presentational devices to effect sporadic audience disengagement.

In Shakespeare's early plays, as I noted above, presentational tactics are used consistently. "Often crudely narrative and histrionically grandiose," as Nevill Coghill notes,[16] soliloquies are distributed indiscriminately to major and minor characters alike to fill in gaps in the action or to give the audience a "précis of events": "The army of the Queen hath got the field; / My uncles both are slain in rescuing me" (*3 Henry VI* 1.4.1–2).

Expository asides, directed sometimes to the audience, sometimes to another character onstage, comment on the action or reveal to the audience the real motives or feeling of the characters. Entrances are carefully accounted for and exits announced in such a way that the audience feels expressly informed about reasons for stage business.[17] A few examples from *3 Henry VI* will make clear the tactical style of these earliest Shakespearean plays.

Act 3, scene 1, for instance, opens with the entrance of two gamekeepers, who, after explaining to themselves why they have come to this spot, see a man entering. They announce: "Here comes a man. Let's stay till he be past." The man is King Henry; not noticing the gamekeepers, he addresses the audience explaining to them that

> My queen and son are gone to France for aid;
> And, as I hear, the great commanding Warwick
> Is thither gone to crave the French king's sister
> To wife for Edward.   (Ll. 28–31)

Many lines later, he is captured by the gamekeepers, and the action (3.2) moves to Edward's court, where Edward's wooing of an English widow is accompanied by a string of "aparts" and "asides":

> WIDOW: Please you dismiss me, either with ay or no.
> KING: Ay, if thou wilt say ay to my request;
>   No, if thou dost say no to my demand.
> WIDOW: Then, no, my lord. My suit is at an end.

RICHARD [aside to Clarence]:
>   The widow likes him not; she knits her brows.
CLARENCE [aside to Richard]:
>   He is the bluntest wooer in Christendom.
KING [aside]: Her looks do argue her replete with modesty;
>   Her words do show her wit incomparable;
>   All her perfections challenge sovereignty.
>   One way or other, she is for a king;
>   And she shall be my love, or else my queen.

(3.2.78–89)

Note, in these exchanges, the patterned, balanced, carefully structured language, typical of formal, presentational drama.

As a final example, act 3 of *3 Henry VI* closes with an explanatory address to the audience by Warwick, who makes clear his new position:

WARWICK: I came from Edward as ambassador,
>   But I return his sworn and mortal foe.
>   Matter of marriage was the charge he gave me,
>   But dreadful war shall answer his demand.

>   .   .   .   .

>   Not that I pity Henry's misery
>   But seek revenge on Edward's mockery.

(3.3.256–265)

When we move to the plays of Shakespeare's middle period (c. 1595–1608), we find a very different use of dramatic tactics. In these representational dramas—those in which he uses the power of language to so control audience imagination that the spectator is given "a representation of life calculated to lift [him] into a realm

45

independent of the theatre and its platform stage" (McCollom, "Formalism and Illusion in Shakespearian Drama," p. 446)—dramatic tactics are very unobtrusive, skillfully woven into the dynamic action and language. Only occasionally do presentational tactics appear. In *As You Like It*, for example, when Oliver first plots against the life of Orlando, or in *King Lear*, when Edmund introduces the Gloucester subplot, Shakespeare has considerable information to impart and much action to initiate, and he uses presentational tactics because they are ready to hand and adequate for his purposes. In each case, he is dealing with a villain who works by hypocrisy and lies; the easiest way to make it clear to the audience that the villain, in the dialogue, is lying, is to have the villain tell us directly that he is not to be trusted. Thus, Oliver and Edmund give openly expository soliloquies—but soliloquies which function quite differently from comparable monologues in *3 Henry VI* or *Cymbeline*.

One major difference is that expository monologues in *King Lear* and *As You Like It* are used, not to tell the story, but simply to give background information or to prepare us for the subsequent action; almost everything of importance in these scenes is translated into dialogue or action, and most of what we learn, we learn through the action itself. In other words, in these scenes, in contrast with *Cymbeline* 1.5, we are "shown" more than we are "told." Edmund tells that he wants his father's land and that he must use trickery to get it; he tells us that the trickery depends on the letter which he holds in his hand. From that point on, dialogue and action take over. The soliloquy lets us know what to watch for in the action—and from then on, we need be "told" nothing. As Edmund allows himself to be "forced" into handing over the letter, we along with Gloucester learn that the handwriting looks like Edgar's: Gloucester, because of

Edmund's clever acting, assumes that Edgar indeed wrote the letter; we, because of the introductory soliloquy, know that the letter must be a forgery. As Gloucester reads the letter aloud, revealing its incriminating suggestions of a plot against his own life, Gloucester himself becomes enraged at the "author" of the letter; we, on the other hand, begin to see what Edmund has in mind; a breach between father and legitimate brother, from which division he himself will prosper. Later in the scene, in the dialogue between Edmund and Edgar, we once again observe intelligent malice as it overcomes innocent credulity, and discover, through the dialogue (which convinces Edgar that his father is angry with him, and that he must stay out of his sight) that the second step in Edmund's plot is to keep Gloucester and Edgar apart, so that Edgar will have no chance to set himself straight with Gloucester. The "tactics" of the scene, then, though the scene contains expository soliloquies, are essentially "representational"; information is conveyed to the audience dynamically, in such a way that suspense continually builds with each new piece of information that is revealed.

In *As You Like It*, the same policy is followed: Oliver tells us in a line or two that he will get rid of Orlando; in a later direct statement to the audience, he says simply " 'Twill be a good way; and tomorrow the wrestling is." From that point on we watch Oliver set his practice in motion as he lies to Charles the Wrestler about Orlando, setting up a situation in which Orlando must certainly be killed. The little expository soliloquies accomplish a necessary function: they give us a proper angle of vision with which to watch Oliver in action; once that angle of vision is established, action takes over, and the story is "rendered," not "told."

In the "wicked queen" scene in *Cymbeline*, the opposite policy is followed: everything of importance is told to us in direct address to

47

the audience, the dialogue centers around untrue assumptions or unnecessary matter, and the "action" of the scene (the transfer of the box of drugs from the doctor to the queen and thence to Pisanio), if the soliloquies and asides remained intact, could well be done in pantomime.

A second major difference between Shakespeare's use of presentational tactics in his representational drama and in his very early and very late drama is the fact that, in the Edmund and Oliver scenes, Shakespeare is careful to limit all soliloquies and asides to a single character, the villain himself (this in sharp contrast to 3 *Henry VI* and to the scene under analysis in *Cymbeline*). In *King Lear* and *As You Like It*, by limiting our subjective view of the action to that of the practicer setting the plot in motion, Shakespeare focuses our attention sharply where it belongs—on the villain and his schemes— and establishes exactly our relation to both villain and victim. The principle at work here is one pointed out by a perceptive film critic, Michael Roemer, who likens the use of soliloquy on the prerealistic stage to the use of montage by the film director. "In the ancient and Elizabethan theatres," he notes, "while we remain in objective possession of the entire stage, the poetry and particularly the soliloquy can focus our attention on one person and shift to his point-of-view. At any given moment, the world can be seen through his eyes, subjectively."[18] The film director can, in the same way, "strengthen the illusion of a primary experience by using the subjective point of view"; can, through the use of montage, "shift from an objective vision of a person to a vision of what he sees," can even "shift from one subjective view to another." In contrast, realistic drama, "with its fidelity to the surfaces of everyday life," is limited to the objective view. "We *know* how Ibsen's Nora sees the world, but except for rare moments we do not *experience* it from her point-of-view. She cannot, as it were, reach out and envelop us in her vision—as Hamlet and Lear can" (Roemer, p. 21).

Soliloquy, then, can focus our attention on the speaker by showing us the action through his eyes. When, as in *Cymbeline* 1.5, three characters address the audience in rapid succession, each giving his view of the action, we get an interesting effect of shifting camera angles, but we are left with no sharp interest in a single character, no heightened expectations in terms of a central person or a single relationship. In the Edmund and Oliver scenes, this focusing, this arousing of suitable expectations, is just what is provided. Oliver addresses us three times, each time rather briefly, giving us just enough insight into his character to make him a clearly suitable comic villain: he is simple, egocentric, hates without reason, schemes with proper alacrity and lack of scruple. His closing soliloquy listing Orlando's virtues is a necessary corrective to the lies he has just told about Orlando in the dialogue and gives us enough information about his brother to arouse the proper hopes about Orlando's ultimate success and rewards.

In *King Lear* Edmund's opening "expository" soliloquy is longer than Oliver's, is more complicated, and is ultimately of more importance. As exposition, it tells us what we need to know about Edmund's character and his motivations and, in common with the monologue which closes the scene, arouses both interest in what is to come and suitable fears about the fate in store for Gloucester and Edgar. But the soliloquy goes far beyond exposition and self-description. The opening lines: "Thou, Nature, art my goddess; to thy law / My services are bound" are indeed presentational and expository; they create little illusion that a "real person" is living before us in a "real world." But as the language of the soliloquy begins to break out of formal patterns of rhythm or logic:

49

> Why brand they us
> With base? with baseness? bastardy? base, base?

the character seems to come alive, and we are caught up into his world:

> Well then,
> Legitimate Edgar, I must have your land.
> Our father's love is to the bastard Edmund
> As to th' legitimate. Fine word—'legitimate'!
> Well, my legitimate, if this letter speed,
> And my invention thrive, Edmund the base
> Shall top th' legitimate.   (1.2.15–21)

In this speech Shakespeare uses the power of language to "inveigle and appasionate the mind" of the audience (to use Puttenham's phrase),[19] and thus pull us into momentary approval of and sympathy for the vicious Edmund. For a moment we are captured by the "psychological vitality" of the man, by his "hard core of character fiercely loyal to itself"[20] and this momentary grasp of Edmund's nature will color our later horror at his actions and add another dimension to the tragedy. Edmund's speech can be classified as an expository soliloquy—a good example, in fact, of the "self-descriptive convention," whereby "the good characters speak of themselves frankly as good and the wicked as wicked" (Stoll, *Shakespeare Studies*, p. 107), but the language, as it becomes introspective and broken, becomes the language of illusion, and the soliloquy pulls us into the play on several levels: it stimulates our interest, it creates strong feelings about Edmund and about his victims, and it lets us know what to watch for in much of the succeeding action.

The scenes from *King Lear* and *As You Like It* would probably never be singled out as examples of "great" Shakespearean scenes.

But they do illustrate the fact that Shakespeare could use presentational conventions in an unobtrusive or even highly dramatic manner. Such is not the case in the *Henry VI* trilogy or in *Cymbeline*. When in *3 Henry VI* all action on the stage stops and Edward informs us, unheard by the numerous characters around him, that Lady Grey "Shall be my love or else my queen," or when in *Cymbeline* the queen breaks off a conversation to say to the audience, "Here comes a flattering rascal; Upon him / Will I first work," convention so intrudes that illusion is destroyed.[21]

When we look again at the tactics of *Cymbeline* 1.5, we seem at first sight to be back in the dramatic world of *3 Henry VI*. In both plays we find self-revealing expository soliloquies, explanatory asides, obtrusive entrance announcements (in *3 Henry VI*, "Here comes a man"; in *Cymbeline*, "Here comes a flattering rascal"). The same "flatness" of language predominates (in *3 Henry VI*, "I came from Edward as ambassador"; in *Cymbeline*, "I do not like her"). The explicitly narrative mode of *3 Henry VI* ("My queen and son are gone to France for aid") is echoed in *Cymbeline* ("I have given him that which . . . shall quite unpeople her"). The bluntness of the asides in *Cymbeline* reminds us of *3 Henry VI*: Richard's "The widow likes him not; she knits her brows" is of the same nature as Cornelius's "I do suspect you, madam, but you shall do no harm." The exit couplets in both plays tend toward doggerel, with Warwick's "Not that I pity Henry's misery, / But seek revenge on Edward's mockery" being actually a bit less awkward than Pisanio's "But when to my good lord I prove untrue / I'll choke myself. There's all I'll do for you."

Yet because of the general styles of the two plays, the tactics have quite different effects. In *3 Henry VI* the very antinaturalism of the tactics brings them into accord with the play's other presentational features—its elaborately grouped entrances and exits, its structured language, its general tendency to face outward toward the audience. In this context, presentational conventions are not disturbing. But in *Cymbeline*, they are disturbing indeed. They are disturbing, in the first place, because the artificiality of the conventions in *Cymbeline* seems deliberately heightened, as if to call our attention to the naiveté of the tactics. By prefacing Cornelius's monologue with four artificial conventions in quick succession (the queen's aside, her exit request, Cornelius's aside, and the "stand aside" request) and by having him dismissed from the stage before and after the monologue, Shakespeare emphasizes the unnaturalness of Cornelius's address and refuses to allow us to overlook this flat, banally expository speech. Pisanio's couplet, too, in spite of Nosworthy's assurances that the bad couplets in this play are just like bad couplets in others of Shakespeare's plays,[22] could only with difficulty be matched in puerility by any of Shakespeare's other writing. Here, again, Shakespeare heightens our awareness of Pisanio's announcement by having him remain obstinately silent throughout the scene in the face of the queen's questions and remarks—until, at last alone onstage, he utters the closing couplet.

The artificiality of certain other "crude" scenes in *Cymbeline* is as obviously pronounced. Two scenes, for instance (1.3 and 2.1), are actually built on a pattern in which every line or so of dialogue is followed by a comment directed toward the audience, as Cloten is twice marched across the stage in converse with his sycophant, followed by the ever-derisive, ever-commenting Second Lord. The second scene built on this pattern of dialogue-with-commentary-asides is climaxed with a redundant expository soliloquy in which the Second Lord summarizes for us Imogen's situation:

> Thou divine Imogen, what thou endur'st,
> Betwixt a father by thy stepdame govern'd,

A mother hourly coining plots, a wooer
More hateful than the foul expulsion is
Of thy dear husband.   (2.1.62–66)

This soliloquy is doubly redundant, since Imogen's situation has been
the sole theme of the play, and needs no comment, and since Imogen
herself had opened the previous scene with a soliloquy covering
exactly the same points:

A father cruel, and a stepdame false;
A foolish suitor to a wedded lady
That hath her husband banish'd.   (1.6.1–3)

Not only the quality, but also the very *quantity* of soliloquies in
Cymbeline emphasizes the artificiality of the convention. In this
play, says Morris Arnold, Shakespeare "out-Herods Herod in pro-
fusion and variety of soliloquies. There are expositions of situation
and character, villainous plottings, explanations of disguise, apostrophes, ragings and lamentations" (*Soliloquies of Shakespeare*,
p. 46). Arnold despairs particularly over those moments in *Cymbeline*
in which Shakespeare resorts to crass storytelling (p. 65)—in which,
that is, "the playwright grows careless of verisimilitude and inserts
long monologs, baldly narrative, for the elucidation of the complicated intrigue. While these were doubtless acceptable to their
audience, they cannot but make the judicious grieve" (p. 72).

Occasionally these "grievous" monologues go beyond mere "bald
narration" and approach the limits of the ludicrous, once again
stressing the artificial. The most infamous of such monologues is the
speech by Belarius in act 3, scene 3. In this scene Belarius and his
two "sons" have made their first entrance into the play, appearing
through the mouth of their cave home. The dialogue makes it clear
that Belarius long ago lived in Cymbeline's court and was banished

thence. Belarius sends the boys off to hunt game, and then begins to speak in soliloquy:

> How hard it is to hide the sparks of nature!
> These boys know little they are sons to th' King;
> Nor Cymbeline dreams that they are alive.
> They think they are mine; and though train'd up thus meanly
> I' th' cave wherein they bow, their thoughts do hit
> The roofs of palaces . . .　　　(3.3.79–84)

We now know that the cave dwellers are Cymbeline's lost sons, Imogen's "thief-stol'n brothers." Belarius goes on for fifteen more lines, telling about the young princes—and then suddenly breaks into an apostrophe to Cymbeline, complete with "the grand style":

> O Cymbeline! heaven and my conscience knows
> Thou didst unjustly banish me;

then follow the flat narrative lines:

> 　　　　　　　　　　whereon,
> At three and two years old, I stole these babes,
> Thinking to bar thee of succession as
> Thou reft'st me of my lands.　　(Ll. 99–103)

Belarius next calls on his dead wife, in the process giving us more information:

> 　　　　　　　　　　Euriphile,
> Thou wast their nurse. They took thee for their mother;

then he switches back to direct address to the audience, with a suitable change to third-person pronouns:

And every day do honour to her grave.
Myself, Belarius, that am Morgan call'd,
They take for natural father. (Ll. 103–107)

As Granville-Barker notes, "we shall have to search far back in Shakespeare's work for anything quite so apparently artless" as this "ingenuously informative . . . *ex post facto* confidence from Belarius" and "may be doubtful of finding it even there."[23]

Yet this obtrusively expository speech is, unlike similar speeches in medieval drama or early Shakespeare, set in a drama that is basically illusive. Hence a second and more important reason that *Cymbeline's* presentational conventions are disturbing. Through scenes of great dramatic tension (cf. the wager scene or the scene of the attempted seduction of Imogen), through emphasis on intense and basic human emotions (grief, anger, jealousy, joy), Shakespeare pulls us into the story-play, makes us identify to some extent with Posthumus, sympathize with Imogen, and feel some concern for Cymbeline and his subjection to the wicked stepmother-queen. Such involvement, such concern, is a necessary part of this play. The core of the play is romance story; its mode is suspense, curiosity, wonder. Instead of formal history, elaborately patterned comedy, or stylized ritual, the play gives us a plethora of story lines: a Snow White tale of a princess, her evil stepmother, a home in the woods and a deathlike sleep; a Romeo-and-Juliet-like tragedy of a banished lover, an unwanted suitor, deaths and near-deaths; a medieval folktale of a chastity-wager and an evil Italian villain—all of these stories centering in the "incomparable Imogen" and all demanding sympathy for the heroine, curiosity about the story endings, and enough suspension of disbelief for us to give the play our attention and interest. In short, the play is primarily representational drama which directs our attention *through* the medium to the story itself.

Further, as I indicated earlier, much of the language of the play is emotionally charged and persuasively real:

> O, for a horse with wings! Hear'st thou, Pisanio?
> He is at Milford Haven . . .
> . . . Then, true Pisanio,
> Who long'st, like me, to see thy lord—who long'st
> (O, let me bate!) but not like me, yet long'st,
> But in a fainter kind—O, not like me!
> For mine's beyond beyond—say, and speak thick
> (Love's counsellor should fill the bores of hearing,
> To th' smothering of the sense), how far it is
> To this same blessed Milford.   (3.2.49ff)

Like Edmund's speech quoted earlier, the very rhythms of Imogen's speech (representative of much of the *Cymbeline* style) break through formality, through metrical and logical restrictions, into intense emotion in order to catch us up into the reality of her world. Lyrically powerful lines combine with coarsely repugnant passages

> This yellow Iachimo in an hour—was't not?
> Or less!—at first? Perchance he spoke not, but,
> Like a full-acorn'd boar, a German one,
> Cried "O!" and mounted.   (2.5.14ff)

> Sluttery, to such neat excellence oppos'd,
> Should make desire vomit emptiness.
>   (1.6.44–45)

>   The cloyed will—
> That satiate yet unsatisfied desire, that tub
> Both fill'd and running—ravening first the lamb,
> Longs after for the garbage.   (1.6.48ff)

56

to create a language style which is intensely emotive. Yet into this language world come presentational tactics in which the language is flattened to comical bluntness ("Here comes a flattering rascal. Upon him / Will I first work. He's for his master / And enemy to my son"),[24] the matter reduced to redundant exposition ("A father cruel and a step-dame false, / A foolish suitor to a wedded lady, / That hath her husband banished") and the artificiality heightened by shifting stylistic levels, bald narration, and ludicrous "apostrophes."

Presentational tactics are not the only presentational devices which intrude startlingly into the predominantly representational style of *Cymbeline*. Lines which remind us that we are watching a play— lines which inevitably make us conscious of ourselves as spectators— are introduced into the play frequently and in an oddly jarring way. The manner in which they appear distinguishes the "artifices" of the Romances from those of such early plays as *Love's Labour's Lost*, where, as Northrop Frye notes, "certain theatrical conventions . . . are used so extravagantly that they parody the conventions" and where "the characters make several references to being in a play" (*A Natural Perspective*, p. 111). In these early sophisticated comedies, little attempt is made to create an illusion of "real life." A play like *Love's Labour's Lost* "holds a mirror up to another mirror, and brings its resolution out of a double illusion" (Frye, p. 111). In *Cymbeline*, in contrast, "artificial" elements interrupt emotionally charged moments, and the effect is jarring. For example, in the final scene of *Cymbeline*, as Norman Rabkin notes, "at one of the emotional climaxes of the final revelations" Posthumus bursts out inexplicably with what Rabkin calls "perhaps the most striking line in the play . . . 'Shall's have a play of this?'" (*Shakespeare and the Common Understanding*, p. 210). (Rabkin could well have quoted the remainder of Posthumus's outbursts, which, accompanying his striking of Imogen/Fidele, continues the play reference: "Thou scornful page / There lies thy part.") Rabkin again notes the incongruity of

> The King's awed expression a moment—and three revelations —later of an attitude he shares with the audience: "New matter still?" . . . Once we have accepted the play's make-believe as make-believe and come to expect no more of it, we are particularly susceptible to the poetic power of a line spoken by a suddenly real and moving Posthumus when Imogen has been restored from her putative death: "Hang there like fruit, my soul / Till the tree die!" (p. 210).

Again, Rabkin might well have continued his analysis by noting that this famous and intensely moving line is followed immediately by another play reference—the king's: "What, mak'st thou me a dullard in this act? / Wilt thou not speak to me?"

Similarly jarring is the juxtaposition of presentational spectacle and stylization with representational "realism." In *Cymbeline* 5.4, Posthumus and the jailer address each other in black-comic prose:

> JAILER: Come, sir, are you ready for death?
> POSTHUMUS: Over-roasted rather; ready long ago.
> JAILER: Hanging is the word, sir. If you be ready for that, you are well cook'd.
> POSTHUMUS: So, if I prove a good repast to the spectators, the dish pays the shot. (Ll. 152–158)

Such realistic prose frames one of drama's most startlingly nonrealistic spectacles—a scene containing "solemn music," ghosts who circle around Posthumus as he sleeps, chanting in ballad rhythm a challenge to Jupiter, and the sudden descent of Jupiter seated on an eagle and throwing a thunderbolt. This inner scene is presentational drama so obtrusively theatrical that it brings the audience close to comic overdistancing; yet it is framed by realistic talk of death and hanging, of hunger and drunkenness, and by such moving comments as Post-humus's:

> And so, great pow'rs,
> If you will take this audit, take this life
> And cancel these cold bonds   (Ll. 26–28)

or his: "I am merrier to die than thou art to live" (l. 176) or the jailer's: "I would we were all of one mind, and one mind good" (ll. 211–212).

According to John Gassner, "Playing cat and mouse with one's sub-ject by spoofing it theatrically . . . may provide entertainment. But playing cat and mouse with the audience by taking it *in* and *out* of the illusion of reality . . . is hardly the way to inspire public con-fidence in a vision or a conviction."[25] Perhaps. But this taking of the audience in and out of the illusion of reality is a precise description of Shakespeare's technique in all three of the plays we are con-sidering.

The Winter's Tale, like *Cymbeline*, is basically representational drama: it tells a story about characters who interest us; its language is thick and illusive, the language of intense passion straining to ex-press itself.[26] Its dramatic tactics are generally more illusive than those in *Cymbeline*—though we cannot forget the intrusion of Father Time, with his stylized rhymed couplets, reminding us that the story of Leontes "actually" happened years ago; nor can we forget the most famous of all Shakespearean exits—startling if the bear is real, amusingly artificial if the bear is a disguised actor.

And S. L. Bethell's comments on the tactical dramaturgy of the sheep-shearing scene—a scene which veers between illusive dialogue, masquelike dances, and antimasque-like antics—are well worth quoting.[27] Bethell suspects that, in *The Winter's Tale*, Shakespeare gives us a "deliberate creaking of the dramatic machinery" (p. 50) and cites that "patch of astonishingly awkward management towards the end of Act IV, scene iv, beginning at the point where Camillo questions Florizel and learns that he is determined to 'put to sea' with Perdita" (4.4.509). Bethell points out the repeated "stand aside" or "go on before" requests, old conventions which allow a character to step forward and address the audience unheard by other characters, and comments:

> Now it is hard to believe that Shakespeare—even if tired, bored, cynical, in despair and dead drunk at the time—could repeat a crudely amateur device like this "talking aside" or "walking before" four times in a few minutes and not intend something by it. Before the end of the scene it has become laughable, and the laugh is increased by the reason Autolycus gives for sending the others ahead (i.e., the necessity of relieving himself); surely, this is a deliberately comic underlining of a deliberately crude technique. (Pp. 49–50)

In *The Winter's Tale*, however, "creaking dramatic tactics" are less important presentational elements than they are in *Cymbeline*. More important in *The Winter's Tale* are the carefully placed dialogue comments about the make-believe nature of the story we are watching.[28] The very title of *The Winter's Tale*, the significance of which is underlined by Mamillius's storytelling scene,

> HERMIONE: Pray you sit by us
>   And tell's a tale.
> MAMILLIUS: Merry, or sad, shall't be?
> HERMIONE: As merry as you will.
> MAMILLIUS: A sad tale's best for winter. I have one
>   Of sprites and goblins.   (2.1.22–26)

places Leontes' tragedy (which is just gathering intensity at this point) in the proper sphere of "sad tales of sprites and goblins" by reminding us that we are watching an old tale "meant to fright us"—but one which must, says Time the Chorus, seem "stale" to the "glistering of this present" (4.1.13). As the play itself becomes most wonderful and strange, we are told that "such a deal of wonder is broken out within this hour that ballad makers cannot be able to express it" (5.2.29), and the improbability of the action (which should "be hooted at like an old tale") is pointed out again and again. The report of what happened to Antigonus is described as "like an old tale still, which will have matter to rehearse, though credit be sleep and not an ear open." The reunion of Paulina and Perdita is described in deliberately theatrical terms: "The dignity of this act was worth the audience of kings and princes, for by such was it acted"; and the final lines of the play uttered by Leontes remind us, if we could indeed have ever forgotten, that we are watching "parts performed":

> Good Paulina,
> Lead us from hence where we may leisurely
> Each one demand, and answer to his part
> Perform'd in this wide gap of time since first
> We were dissever'd.   (5.3.151ff.)

And spectacle, too, is important in *The Winter's Tale*—no Jupiter descending on an eagle in thunder and lightning, but a statue which comes to life at the sound of music and at the command of the masque-presenter, Paulina. In this scene (as in the spectacle scene in *Cymbeline*), the very formal language of

> Music! awake her! strike!
> 'Tis time; descend; be stone no more; approach;

Strike all that look upon with marvel. Come;

I'll fill your grave up!   (5.3.98–101)

is followed by such moving outbursts as Leontes' "Oh, she's warm!"

In *The Tempest* the most important presentational devices are the spectacles. Other presentational devices do appear: the frequent mention of "three or four hours" of time passing on the island, for instance, may be seen as deliberate reminders that, in *The Tempest*, Shakespeare is obtrusively observing, indeed, "flaunting," the classical unities; Prospero's "long narrative to the drowsily obedient Miranda" may be viewed as comically tedious, a burlesque of stage exposition;[29] certainly Prospero's famous speech on the dissolving of the revels (as well as his role of stage manager throughout) reminds us that we are watching a play. But it is the spectacles which most often distance us from Prospero's world. At the climax of each subplot of *The Tempest*, as Frank Kermode notes, "there is a spectacular contrivance that owes something to masque: the rapacity of the three men of sin is confronted by its own image in the allegorical figure of the Harpy; the disorderly desires of Caliban and his confederates are chastised, Acteon-like, by hounds; and the betrothal of Ferdinand and Miranda is marked by a courtly mythological entertainment."[30] And Kermode (as well as Stephen Orgel and Enid Welsford)[31] likens Prospero to a masque-presenter under whose spell the castaways wander helpless until he chooses to release them.

Spectacle is admittedly theatrical: it is "presented" for "spectators." Its intrusion into representational drama creates an audience dislocation comparable to that created by presentational tactics or obtrusive references to the play. Yet the story told in *The Tempest* is a romance story of young love, attempted murder, revenge, and mercy; except for the moments of spectacle, we are led to take this story as somehow "real." The language of the poetry, the interplay of characters, the individual dramatic incidents are not part of an allegorical masque, but are illusively dramatic. In this context the spectacles (which, in each case, break into the action startlingly and disappear abruptly) alter the quality of our awareness, make us conscious of the fictive nature of the entire play. Because Prospero's position is analogous to that of the masque hero (in that he and the audience share an awareness of the fictive nature of the play world)[32] the distance between stage and audience in *The Tempest* is more consistent than in the other Romances, and the tactical dramaturgy has, as a result, less often been criticized. But the spectacles in *The Tempest*, like those in the other last plays, are no more a natural part of representational drama than are the presentational conventions of *Cymbeline*.

To use an analogy from painting: in the Romances Shakespeare gives us pictures which seem to be "relational models" of the real world (that is, they can be read in terms of recognizable resemblances to extraartistic reality) into which he introduces distortions which interfere with that very reading.[33] In his early plays the distortions away from reality are consistent so that the microcosm created allows of a coherent reading; in the plays of the late 1590s and early 1600s, distortions are essentially eliminated. In the last plays, distortions force us to reexamine any reading which equates the plays with the real world. The representational moments in the Romances seem to us very "real" indeed; then, suddenly, with the intrusions of presentational conventions, of references to the play world, or of spectacle, we are forced out of these "real" worlds into theatrical worlds of artificial entrances and exits, fiction, or spectacular contrivance, and the plays become "living drolleries." Just as suddenly, the theatrical moment passes, and once again we are caught up in the play world, listening to passionate, illusive language.

Along with the blending of tragedy and comedy, then, violent con-

junctions of representational and presentational styles characterize the
Romances and set them apart from Shakespeare's other plays. This is
not to say that Shakespeare had not before blended theatrical styles;
indeed, the blending of the formal (presentational) and the illusive
(representational) occurs in all great drama; the tensions thus set up
no true dramatist would try to avoid. Yet in most of Shakespeare's
plays, his touch is light and sure; in the Romances, the two styles
blend bewilderingly and shockingly as we are repeatedly taken *in*
and *out* of the illusion of reality.[34]

The question now remains: why should Shakespeare have chosen to
shape the tactical dramaturgy of the Romances so strangely? Since
this question is intimately tied up with questions to be considered
in later chapters, a final answer will have to wait until other strands
in the pattern become clearer. But we can here point to at least two
effects which the chosen tactical dramaturgy creates. First, the stories
told in the Romances are deliberately and delightfully implausible;
on the surface, they are entertainments, complete with Italian villains,
magic islands, music, and improbable reunions. Yet they deal with
serious human emotions, with suffering and loss and death. To maintain the delicate response necessary for enjoyment of these stories
Shakespeare blends his theatrical styles, in effect refusing to let us
take the characters or the actions too seriously. On this level, the
blending of styles relates closely to the blending of tragedy and
comedy examined in chapter 1. It relates as well to the effect noted
by several critics: namely, by deliberately displaying the fictiveness of
his Romance world, Shakespeare heads off attacks of "implausibility,"
and says to us, in effect, "I never claimed this play was more than a
fiction." Thus disarmed, we can respond fully to the delight and
wonder of the final revelations and reunions.

Second, and on a deeper level, by sporadically and jarringly breaking the dramatic illusion, Shakespeare creates for the audience a distinctive kind of dramatic experience—an experience interestingly parallel to the experience of the characters on stage. For the audience, characters in whom we are encouraged to believe suddenly turn into puppets; suspenseful dramatic actions begin to build, only to be swept away by theatrical spectacle; the audience becomes increasingly involved emotionally until a quick line of dialogue reminds us that we are only watching a fiction. The experience (when the play is sensitively read or staged) is a complex one, in which we are repeatedly and rudely awakened from a compelling dream.[35]

For the characters a similar complexity prevails as "reality" and "illusion" blur bewilderingly. Characters continually confuse waking and dreaming. Imogen wakes from her sleep/death believing that her experience in the Welsh mountains was only a dream, " 'Twas but a bolt of nothing, shot at nothing, / Which the brain makes of fumes." She hopes that the headless man beside her is a dream, but finds that "The dream's here still. Even when I wake it is / Without me, as within me; not imagin'd, felt" (4.2.299–307). Hermione knows that Leontes is living a waking nightmare, knows that her life "stands in the level of [his] dreams," and is told that her actions *are* his dreams—that she "had a bastard by Polixenes" and Leontes "but dreamed it"—a frightening statement of the truth intended as sarcasm. And Ferdinand is far from the only character in *The Tempest* whose "spirits, as in a dream, are all bound up."

To add to the complexity, untruths and illusions provide the bases for most of the actions in these plays. Throughout the plays, characters act in terms of falsely held beliefs: in *Cymbeline*, for example, Imogen is not unfaithful and she is not killed by Pisanio; thus Posthumus's intense actions and reactions throughout the play have no basis in fact. Imogen's journey to Milford-Haven is posited on a false belief that she goes to join Posthumus; her joining of the Roman army is posited on another false belief—that is, that Posthumus is dead. In *The Winter's Tale* Leontes falsely believes Hermione unchaste; later, he falsely believes her dead and spends sixteen years grieving for a woman who is in fact alive, as well as for a living daughter also thought dead. In *The Tempest* all that happens to the Court Party and the mariners is based on illusion—as Prospero constantly reminds us. The wreck itself was but an illusion; the banquet is an illusion; the Harpy, the masque, the spirit-hounds, the very music that lures Ferdinand and the drunken sailors are illusory, created by Ariel, who is himself "but air."

Further, it is the untruths, the illusions, which call up not only the most significant actions, but also the most intense emotions from the characters. Alonso's powerful speech of remorse and repentance, for example, is brought about by the illusion of the Harpy and by a lie about Ferdinand's death—that is, his remorse and despair are real, even through the person for whom he grieves is not "bedded in the ooze." Imogen's intense emotional reactions—joy at the prospect of joining Posthumus, grief at finding beside her the headless body of Posthumus—grow out of untruths, as does the lovely dirge spoken over the dead body of Fidele: Fidele is not dead. Antigonus's decision to abandon Perdita in Bohemia, and his long speech of despair, grief, tenderness all grow out of a series of illusions brought to him significantly by a dream. Further, at the conclusions of the plays, when the falsehoods are replaced by truths, the characters discover that even their larger assumptions have been untrue, and that the force shaping the action is not what they had believed: not Chance, but Jupiter; not so much Apollo as Paulina (with the help from Camillo and Autolycus); not Fate or accident, but Prospero, long thought dead.

Throughout these plays, then, the characters seldom act in terms of "reality"—nor are we led to believe that they *could*. They act in terms of what they are given, and, to repeat, most often their most intense emotional outpourings or their most desperate actions are based on untruths. And when the clouds of illusion are cleared away, it is seldom because of rational action or because of taking care; rather, it is because Jupiter has decided that it is time for happiness to prevail, or because Camillo has decided to return home, or because Prospero has decided that the rarer action is in virtue rather than in vengeance. And because we ourselves are treated by Shakespeare as the characters in these plays are treated by Jupiter, Paulina, or Prospero—sporadically deceived and undeceived, pulled into and out of belief—we are placed in a unique relationship to the experience of the characters in the play, and can feel the full implications of the fantastic complexity of the appearance/reality problem. Because our dramatic response is that "sporadic engagement and detachment" noted earlier, we as an audience can personally sense the full implications of the fact that one can never truly separate illusion from reality, can never be truly certain that his actions are rational, his emotions rationally based, his beliefs certain and lasting. Thus we are forced into a complex awareness of life: we believe and do not believe; we act but cannot rationally defend our actions.

These plays, then, may be "metadramas"; they may be "deliberately artificial"—but not, as even some of the best critics suggest, because Shakespeare was solely interested in play-making. Granted that, in *Cymbeline*, for example, "Shakespeare's game is to engage us in the naïve artifice of the piece, to make us believe its reality, and then to make us recognize the game he is playing" (Rabkin, *Shakespeare and the Common Understanding*, p. 211). Yet this does not make of *Cymbeline* a play concerned solely with play-making, a play with the "odd and . . . disappointing theme" that Rabkin finds as "the sum of what Shakespeare has to say" in it: namely, that "the world of tragedy can be redeemed in *Cymbeline* . . . simply because the playwright can deny its tragic inevitability by his power over the plot" (p. 211). Nor is *Cymbeline* the failure that Howard Felperin essentially finds it—a play which "is finally the victim of its own romantic unity, a unity of design so tight that it effectively seals off the play from the world we know" (*Shakespearean Romance*, p. 196). Rather, *Cymbeline*, like the other Romances, springs from a deep Shakespearean center, and its strangeness, like that of the other Romances, speaks directly to us about the strangeness of the world which we know through our own experience. The *mimesis* is admittedly subtle—but the world of the Romances, including *Cymbeline*, is very much our world.

CHAPTER III

"So Like an Old Tale":
Dramatic Strategy in the Romances

When we look closely at the structures of Shakespeare's Romances—
at the way he arranges his scenes, develops his situations, tells his
stories—we realize that in strategy as in tactics,[1] these plays are
strange creations. Each of them is vaguely reminiscent of one of the
three "patterns" which Bernard Beckerman finds in the Globe plays:[2]
Cymbeline reminds us of the "river pattern," with its tributary actions
flowing together near the play's end; *The Winter's Tale* is a version
of the "mirror pattern," with the second half of the play reflecting
(by similarities and contrasts) the first half; and *The Tempest*
resembles the "episodic pattern," with the play cutting from one
isolated story line to another. Yet the plays differ sharply from earlier
Shakespearean structures—not only in that each of them is "cyclic,"
as Clifford Leech has demonstrated,[3] but also in that each varies from
its "Globe play" pattern in interestingly significant ways. In each,
the usual Shakespearean midplay climax is missing, as is the normal
Shakespearean curve of expectation-fulfillment; in each, numerous
important narrative devices appear. As a result of these variations on
earlier structures, the Romances give us plays as much like "old
tales" as like dramas. Their potency comes as much from the power
of story as from the very different power of drama.

To understand how Shakespeare achieved this remarkable effect in
his Romances, we need to study these variations, for it is in the
variations that the Romances find their structural similarities. First,
the avoidance of the midplay climax: we may assign to the word
climax any of its current definitions: the point of marked emotional

intensification (or, as Beckerman prefers, the "plateau" of such emotional intensity); the point of open conflict and maximum complication (the "Epitasis, or busie part of our subject," as Ben Jonson called it); or the turning point in the action (the Aristotelian *peripeteia*, translated by Fredson Bowers, in terms of Shakespearean dramaturgy, as that moment at which the comic or tragic outcome of the drama is determined).[4] However we define it, the characteristic Shakespearean drama carefully leads up to, and away from, such a climax, while the last plays just as carefully avoid any such pyramidal structure.

In *Twelfth Night* (which we may use as our example of a typical "river pattern" drama) we notice that Shakespeare uses the merging of the various streams of dramatic action to create a climax of extreme "busienesse" and open complication. As Beckerman points out (pp. 50–51) the two main dramatic actions (the Viola-Olivia-Orsino sequence and the Malvolio-Toby-Andrew sequence) "flow independently through the first two acts"; the third stream (the Sebastian-Antonio sequence), "merely a trickle until it joins the main flow," enters the main action in 3.4. With the converging of the tributary actions, suddenly and dramatically, a climactic plateau of intense activity and comic confusion emerges, all leading to the "turning point" climax: Sebastian's subjection to Olivia's charms. At this point the happiness of Viola is assured: a husband has been provided for Olivia; Viola—with her brother returned—can reveal herself as herself, and her marriage to Orsino is certain to follow.[5]

In the Shakespearean "mirror pattern" drama, in contrast, the climax is differently handled. Instead of tributary actions merging to create conflict, complications, and *peripeteia*, we have the various plots acting separately to create intense midplay action. In *King Lear*, for instance, the climactic plateau stretches over the entire third act, as the main plot of Lear and his daughters and the mirror plot of

Gloucester and his sons reach moments of highest intensity and deepest despair in the madness of Lear on the heath (3.2, 4, 6) and in the blinding of Gloucester (3.7). The "turning" of the play's action toward its final issue occurs in the third act scenes interspersed with the madness and blinding scenes, those scenes (3.3, 5) in which Edmund betrays his father and, in his treachery, achieves a position of power and consolidates the forces against Lear, Gloucester, and Cordelia. The entire third act is one of supreme tragic intensity from which the remaining tragic outcome results with seeming inevitability.

The "episodic pattern" achieves an effect of climax in yet another way. Both Beckerman and Marco Mincoff characterize the actions of *Hamlet* and *Macbeth* as "episodic" in that the structure in each case is essentially serial, the dramatic events semiautonomous, with each complication more or less solved as it arises.[6] In plays of the episodic type, the effect of a triangular rise-and-fall action results, says Mincoff, from Shakespeare's careful control of emotional tension to create a rhythmic pulsation; the events are linked in sequence, each event in turn reaching a higher emotional intensity until we reach the apex in midplay. (Beckerman's explanation is much the same. On the basic narrative progression, which tells the story of what happens to the characters, Shakespeare imposes a dramatic progression, which concentrates on what the main character undergoes; it is this dramatic progression, extending to the height of passion at the center of the play, which gives us a climactic midplay plateau.) Mincoff describes the *Macbeth* structure as a series of "strong, rapid pulsations," rising to a sort of climax with the murder of Duncan, falling again "with a single pulse beat—the discovery of the murder—down to the news of Macbeth's election," then rising again to the banquet scene, "the true climax, in which Macbeth appears for the first time at the full height of his glory" and "at the same moment loses his nerve and becomes an object of suspicion to his thanes." "By skillful combination of these two points with the high emotional tension of the Ghost's appearance," notes Mincoff, "an apex is formed that almost miraculously outtops the peak of Duncan's murder" (p. 64).

We can trace a similar "centering and emotional stressing of the turn of the action" (Mincoff, p. 65) in such simply structured episodic plays as *Julius Caesar*, as well as in such complex structures as that of *Hamlet*, where the climactic plateau extends throughout the third act, reaching its highest point of intensity, and its *peripeteia*,[7] in the closet scene.

If we turn now to the Romances, we see a very different dramatic strategy at work. In *Cymbeline*, for example, which is reminiscent of "river pattern" drama, we should expect, in midplay, a sudden grand conflux of tributary actions, a sudden outburst of confusion and activity, and (rising out of it all), the first indication that Imogen's purity will finally be established, Iachimo punished, and Posthumus and Imogen reunited. Indeed, as we begin the midplay action, some such climactic plateau seems to be developing. But instead of a convergence at Milford-Haven—a coming together of stories and characters—we get a slackening of the dramatic tension as Posthumus and Iachimo disappear from the story, Pisanio decides not to kill Imogen, and Imogen herself wanders into a new locality and into a new story. The midplay action, then, gives us, instead of converging story lines and open conflict, the beginnings of two new stories which effectually usurp the interest hitherto borne by the wager plot and the unwanted suitor plot. And, instead of some indication at this point that Imogen's name will be cleared and her happiness with Posthumus assured, we get only a temporary reprieve from Posthumus's anger (in Pisanio's refusal to kill Imogen) and (in the discovery of the lost heirs) the first signs that Cymbeline's family may eventually be reunited.

In *The Winter's Tale*, too, the usual midplay climax is replaced by a slackening of tension. Instead of two plots reaching a peak of intensity, we have the apparent conclusion of one plot and the beginning of the second. We do, admittedly, get a midplay scene of open conflict and emotional intensity: in the trial scene (3.2), Leontes accuses Hermione, she defends herself, and the oracle is read and denied. But the conflicts of this crisis action, instead of giving an impetus to action in acts 4 and 5, appear to be resolved within the scene itself with Mamillius's death, Hermione's reported death, and Leontes' grief-stricken repentance. And the scenes which follow serve to reinforce our feeling that the trial scene (the climactic scene of "the Leontes-story") is also its denouement. Looking back on the trial scene from the vantage point of the final action of the play, we may find hints that complications resolved at the last were suggested in midplay; but in the midplay action itself, only the discovery of the baby by the shepherd gives us any hope that eventual happiness is in store for Leontes, and there is no suggestion that the drama could possibly end with Hermione's return. Further, the midplay deaths, the shifts of time and locale, the appearance of Father Time and the introduction of a new story line all seem deliberately designed to undercut the sustained emotional intensity of the normal climactic plateau.

A like effect of undercutting, or blunting, of the central climax is achieved in *The Tempest*, with several factors operative. First, in act 3 of *The Tempest*, instead of a single action moving rhythmically toward a crisis, each of the three story lines is touched on in turn, each in "another part of the island"; only the Court Party plot reaches a moment of high intensity during this midplay action, but this climax (the scene of the Harpy and the disappearing banquet) comes suddenly on us, not as the apex of several events of progressively rising emotional intensity (as in *Hamlet* or *Macbeth*), but as an unexpected visit from the supernatural. Second, the repentance of Alonso during this scene, though perhaps critical in determining Prospero's later forgiveness of the "men of sin," has no immediate dramatic impact, in that Alonso's desperate reaction suggests no turning of the action toward a happy or unhappy ending.

More important than either of these factors, though, is the curiously distanced role which Prospero plays during this section of the play. Instead of becoming increasingly involved in the action in midplay (as is customary for the hero of "episodic pattern" dramas), Prospero almost disappears from the stage. When we do see him in act 3, he is "at a distance," or "above, invisible." His detachment here lends a strangely distanced quality to that part of the play that is usually the most actively dramatic in Shakespearean drama. When Prospero again enters the drama in an active role, in act 4, the play is reaching its conclusion. As the play gathers intensity in the two concluding scenes, Prospero's role is more and more heavily elaborated,[8] but in the central section of the play, his detachment from the action strips the normal climactic plateau of almost all intensity, turning even the Harpy scene to a "living drollery."

In *Cymbeline*, *The Winter's Tale*, and *The Tempest* then we find a common avoidance, displacement, or blunting of the normal Shakespearean midplay climax. This fact is in two ways significant. In the first place Shakespeare's method of handling the climactic moment—the point of the turning action—in each of his plays is always of importance, always an indication of the underlying dramatic purposes of the play. As Fredson Bowers reminds us, if one isolates the turning point of any of Shakespeare's plays and examines Shakespeare's method of dramatizing that climactic moment, one will have determined the major significance of the plot and an important part of the play's total meaning.[9] Shakespeare's sudden presentation, then, in his Romances, of three plays which seem each to avoid any normal turning-point action, any feeling of midplay climactic intensity or significant complication, cannot fail to arouse our critical interest.

In the second place Shakespeare's avoidance here of the midplay climax is significant in that it is, in effect, a refusal to cast these stories into the normal dramatic frame. Such a refusal seems curiously perverse—or incredibly careless. A major problem facing the Elizabethan dramatist was the casting into dramatic form of romantic narrative—the presenting of stories filled with adventure and variety, covering much time and many places, in a form suitable for stage presentation, a form necessarily concentrated and limited.[10] As I mentioned earlier, the solution, according to Beckerman, was the imposition on the narrative line of a dramatic progression which reaches its highest point in midplay with the hero's maximum involvement in the tragic or comic situation and with the foreshadowing of the hero's fate in the turning-point action. For Beckerman, Shakespeare's architectonic superiority is indicated by the marked intensity of the center of action of his plays; few other Elizabethan dramas achieve that "rich florescence that makes the center of a Shakespearean play such an overwhelming dramatic experience" (Beckerman, p. 45). Yet the Romances, in large part, remove the hero from the play's center action, and avoid this intense midplay activity. The result is that the controlling dramatic frame is missing, and we are left with the narrative line alone. Complication, intensity, and decisive action are saved for the denouement, and we are thrown, in *The Winter's Tale* and *Cymbeline*, suddenly back into that pre-Shakespearean dramatic form foreshadowed by the sprawling Digby *Mary Magdalen*[11] and ridiculed by Sidney[12]—and, in *The Tempest*, into a strangely nondramatic, masquelike form. Had Shakespeare produced his Romances early in his career,[13] we could, in fact, easily explain their curiously nondramatic quality in terms of a medieval romance-play heritage not yet outgrown.

The destruction of dramatic form and intensity resulting from Shakespeare's avoidance of the midplay climax is augmented by the second structural feature which the Romances have in common, namely, the breaking down of the normal Shakespearean expectation-fulfillment pattern. Most great drama depends upon the power of an anticipation-fulfillment curve to create what Susanne Langer calls the "peculiar intensity known as dramatic quality."[14] Consequently, most dramatists seek to place the audience in a state of awareness superior to that of the participants in the drama; they seek to propel us into and through the play by creating a tension between the present moment and the future which the drama creates before our eyes. For this end, they select words, acts, and characters to shape a situation pregnant with its own complications and its own dimly shadowed resolution; they control circumstances so that the dramatic situation "grows to its climax . . . branching into elaborate detail in the course of its development, and in the end . . . [is] resolved by the closing of the action."[15] The great dramatists fulfill our expectations so skillfully that in the very gratification there is an element of surprise, and in the most painful of tragic ends a pleasure in the fulfillment of what we had so long foreseen. Shakespeare is acknowledged to be supreme among the masters of such dramatic strategy, and one could argue that it is in his control of audience expectation and fulfillment that Shakespeare's dramatic genius most clearly manifests itself.

Yet, in his last plays, Shakespeare suddenly departs from the usual expectation patterns we have learned to associate with his drama. Although, as John Lawlor points out,[16] the endings of the Romances fulfill desires which Shakespeare subtly plants in us and for which we hardly dare hope, the plays are structured so that we ourselves are kept unaware of growing patterns. Shakespeare omits the usual preparatory speeches and scenes, he gives occasional bits of misleading information, he arranges circumstances so that one piece of action prepares us for no particular action as a consequence. Instead of following his customary policy of "turning the arrows of our desires in a certain direction and then setting the plot in motion in the direction of these arrows,"[17] he often leads us astray or springs on us some action for which we are totally unprepared. The effect created is that of wonder and surprise, rather than of fulfilled expectations.

The Winter's Tale is the most notorious of the plays in regard to foiled expectations. Nowhere else in the Shakespeare canon are we— along with the dramatis personae—misled into thinking that a leading character is dead, and left in this state of misapprehension throughout much of the play. Shakespeare's sudden departure here from his policy of never lying to the audience has so puzzled critics that explanations for this unique feature of The Winter's Tale abound.[18] Perhaps, critics say, Shakespeare's decision to restore Hermione to life was made at the last minute, so that when he wrote act 3, he still intended to follow his source and end the play with Perdita's return and Leontes' death; or, perhaps Shakespeare wrote a crucial expository scene—now lost—which, placed between the present scenes 2 and 3 of act 3, would advise us of the truth about Hermione's survival.

Such suggestions ignore the fact that Hermione's resurrection is only one of many surprises in this play. Bertrand Evans's comment about the un-Shakespearean strategy of the preparation for the trial scene—"instead of reassuring us, he has avoided obvious means of reassurance" (Shakespeare's Comedies, p. 269)—is applicable to much of the play; we are simply unprepared for many of the major incidents. Leontes' sudden rage of jealousy, Mamillius's death, Hermione's "death," the bear which springs on stage to devour Antigonus, the sudden storm which destroys a shipload of men, all are unexpected and startling.[19] More significantly, we are more than once actually misled about the play's action. In the opening scene, we are carefully prepared for action which will center on the friendship of Leontes and Polixenes and on the young prince Mamillius. The fact that the expository scene never mentions Hermione, that the celebrated friendship immediately explodes into attempted murder, and that Mamillius, about whom much of the opening exposition centers, simply disappears from the action and dies, is almost as startling—in terms of Shakespeare's normal dramaturgical practices—as is the later deliberate deception of the audience concerning Hermione's death. This deception is only an exaggerated form of milder deceptions practiced on the audience throughout the play, just as the sense of wonder accompanying her revival is an enlarging of the many moments of surprise or delight that the play provides.

In *Cymbeline*, instead of misleading the audience, Shakespeare so arranges his interwoven plot lines that larger expectation patterns about the play's action are never allowed to develop. The succession of incidents is made to seem arbitrary and whimsical. Posthumus, in exile, accidentally meets Iachimo, and the wager plot is set in motion. Imogen, fleeing from her husband's wrath, meets her brothers, and later Lucius, by accident. As Clifford Leech puts it: "The coming together of all the characters in Act V, with Iachimo's repentance and confession, the Queen's death and confession, and Cymbeline's decision to make a peace favourable to his conquered enemies, is the contrivance of Fortune or of Providence, not the simple conclusion from the play's premises" ("The Structure of the Last Plays," p. 23). When incidents occur as Fortune or Chance (or a whimsical Jupiter) directs, expectations cannot grow as they do in Shakespearean dramas where one action causes another. In the absence of a growing, developing, encompassing dramatic action, we (like the characters in the play) must simply experience each event as it occurs, waiting for the outcome and the significance of the story to be revealed in the fullness of time.

In *Cymbeline*, as in *The Winter's Tale*, the breakdown of the larger expectation pattern is echoed in smaller strategic details. Iachimo does his evil work and then disappears from the action until the denouement. He alone holds the key to Imogen's happiness, and, as Bertrand Evans notes, as far as we know he leaves the world of the play never to return (*Shakespeare's Comedies*, p. 262). In contrast, say, with the strategy of *Much Ado about Nothing*, where, when Hero is shamed, we know that counterforces have already been set in motion by the arrest of Borachio, we are left throughout much of *Cymbeline* with no idea of how Imogen's name can ever be cleared.

Again, in preparing for the crucial "bedroom scene" in *Cymbeline*, Shakespeare departs widely from his normal strategic policies. He gives us no advanced warning that Iachimo is a villain; he lets us believe (in 1.6) that Iachimo has given up hope of winning his wager; he drops no hint that Iachimo will hide in a trunk in Imogen's bedroom. As Bertrand Evans points out, when Iachimo, at the end of 1.6, "turns as with an afterthought" to request Imogen to guard his trunk for him, "it is made to appear *to us as to Imogen* that his new request has no possible connection with what has just passed. . . . Since we are not to see Iachimo again until he emerges from the trunk beside Imogen's bed," says Evans, "we should ordinarily expect him to linger at the end of the scene in order to explain his intentions. But he leaves with Imogen without so much as a smirk for our advisement."

Evans continues:

The omission contradicts Shakespeare's method in every play until now. Usually, we would have been advised explicitly even earlier—when Iachimo seemed to give up his hope of winning the wager—that he would shift from an honest test of Imogen's virtue to some treacherous device; next, at the conclusion of the scene with Imogen, he would have remained for a moment to tell us plainly that he would enter the bedchamber in the trunk. . . . As the scenes are actually devised, however, not only is the usual care to make assurance double sure omitted, but the least suggestion that Iachimo will enter the trunk is avoided. (*Shakespeare's Comedies*, p. 257)

The significant point about the "trunk device," notes Evans, "is that Shakespeare has not told us what to expect"—he has "denied us" the usual advance notice. When Iachimo suddenly appears out of the trunk by Imogen's bed, the effect is one of total surprise for the audience. This effect of total surprise, which occurs often in both *Cymbeline* and *The Winter's Tale*, is almost unknown in Shakespearean drama outside of the Romances.

In *The Tempest*, too, we are repeatedly startled (usually by intrusions of the supernatural into the natural world), and, as in the other Romances, we are never allowed to build any larger expectation patterns about the play's action: not because we are misled (as in *The Winter's Tale*), nor because the lines of action seem whimsical and fortuitous (as in *Cymbeline*), but because the action of the play is made to seem the result of Prospero's mind—and he alone appears to know what is happening, why, and how. Instead of an action growing inevitably out of an initial situation, Prospero himself seemingly creates the situation and controls its development step by step.

Unlike other "manipulating" characters in Shakespeare's plays, Prospero seems larger than the action, larger than the audience. Rosalind, Hamlet, Richard III, Edmund, Iago—each gets joyful, grim, or diabolic pleasure from his temporary "playing" of other people. Yet in each of the plays in which these characters appear, the spectator is placed in a position of awareness such that the "manipulator" seems swept along by an action larger than any "stage manager" included in the play.

Not so with Prospero and *The Tempest.* Prospero throughout sees far more than we do; like Miranda, we must be told what is happening, and our innocent bewilderment is often much like hers. Prospero realizes that his hour has come to act, and he seems to know exactly what he intends to do; but we must simply wait and watch as his plot unfolds before us. Occasionally he lets us overhear his instructions to Ariel; more often, he tells Ariel "in his ear" what task he must now perform, and we are as surprised as is Miranda when Ferdinand is led dazedly onstage, as startled as is Alonso when a banquet and Harpy appear.

In the Ferdinand and Miranda plot, Prospero does prepare us for much of the action and allow us to build up expectations which are subsequently fulfilled. In the two parallel actions, however, we are kept generally ignorant of what Prospero has in mind. We know that he has much to do, and that time is limited, but specific information is fed to us only piecemeal, whenever Prospero chooses to give us a word of explanation. At the end of the Harpy scene, for example, Prospero tells us that his enemies are now in his power, but drops no hint about what he plans to do with them; only later, at Ariel's urging, does he say that he plans to forgive them. In this plot line, in particular, we must, from beginning to end, simply watch alertly, trusting that Prospero, hard at work in his cave, or observing "from a distance" or "on top," has all under control. This manipulative function of Prospero (his ability to interrupt any situation at will, to bring the *dramatis personae* under his absolute power—to wake them, put them to sleep, paralyze their arms or brains, lead them about the island as he pleases, to create visions, storms, at a thought) and, more important, his second function as author surrogate—that of holding in his own mind the time schedule of the action so that an event which comes suddenly upon us is, for him, "perform'd exact," as he commanded "to th' syllable"—prevents our building up any larger expectations and gives to *The Tempest* a strangely nondramatic quality.[20]

Harold Wilson comments at length on the nondramatic quality of *The Tempest* in his comparison of this play with *Measure for Measure*. The plays are alike in their use of a "directing duke," but *The Tempest*, he finds, is less a play than it is "a succession of magic spells accompanied by the magician's interpretive comments."[21] It is "less dramatic, less deeply moving" than *Measure for Measure*. The difference between the two plays he attributes to the fact that Prospero "takes us immediately into his confidence and explains his purpose as he goes along" while "Duke Vincentio never explicitly states his purpose . . . and we are left to deduce it from the course and outcome of the action." In *The Tempest* ("largely spectacle, filled with tableaux, music, dances, and some of the finest poetry Shakespeare ever wrote"), the action and thought of the play are "made crystal clear in Prospero's explanations"; this in contrast to the more straightforwardly dramatic, more deeply stirring *Measure for Measure*, a play in which "the action contains the thought" (pp. 278–279).

I have quoted Wilson's discussion of *The Tempest* at some length, not because I agree with it completely—we have already seen, for instance, that Prospero does not always make things "crystal clear" or take us "immediately into his confidence"—but because Wilson's comments do indicate a function of Prospero's role which has great bearing on our consideration of the Romances as a whole. For Wilson is correct in noting that Prospero does explain, does interpret, does "tell" us a large part of his story. Although Prospero, as author surrogate, refuses to establish for the audience a sense of the design of the action, a feeling of anticipation or foreboding which would give unity to the succession of scenes presented, Prospero, as expositor, interpreter, and explainer of the action, does take on a "narrative" function that provides a new kind of unity which *The Tempest* shares with *The Winter's Tale* and *Cymbeline.*[22]

This unity is essentially "narrative" unity, and the persistent use of narrative devices in the last plays—the third structural feature which these plays have in common—is in large part responsible for the characteristic quality of the plays. Most of the attacks on late Shakespearean dramaturgy focus on these narrative devices: the narrator in *The Winter's Tale* is "pure fake" (Shakespeare, "having proposed to himself a drama in which a wronged woman has to bear a child, who has to be lost for years and restored to her as a grown girl, simply did not know how to do it, save by invoking some such device"); the narrated recognition scene (*The Winter's Tale* 5.2) is "a serious scamping of artistry," a "laxity of construction, of workmanship" ("In proportion as we have paid our tribute to the art of the story by letting our interest be intrigued, our emotions excited, are we not cheated when Shakespeare lets us down with this reported tale?");[23] the narrative monologues which abound in *Cymbeline* are "redundant," "flat," "a disintegrating change" from mature Shakespearean writing,[24] and Prospero as narrator adds a note of "comic tedium" to *The Tempest* with his "long narrative to the drowsily obedient Miranda," and throughout the play undercuts the dramatic intensity by explaining and interpreting too freely.[25]

That Shakespeare might deliberately have introduced narrative structural devices into these plays, might actually have sought the effects of narrative within the dramatic mode, has not been seriously studied. Yet, if we look closely at these narrative devices—at the chorus and narrated recognition scene in *The Winter's Tale,* at the

expository and commentary monologues in *Cymbeline*, at the extensive explanations and interpretations of Prospero in *The Tempest*—
it is hard to view them as other than carefully controlled structural
elements. Not only do they serve the function (as discussed in chapter 2, above) of breaking the dramatic illusion by increasing the
aesthetic distance; but they also serve a narrative function quite in
keeping with the structural characteristics of these plays. The breaking
down of dramatic form in the Romances through the blunting of the
midplay climax and the shattering of the expectation-fulfillment patterns leave these plays in need of structural devices to provide the
continuity, commentary, and unity normally provided by the dramatic
form itself; by giving continuity and commentary to the last plays,
the above-noted narrative devices perform this necessary service,
replacing the missing dramatic unity and intensity with an essentially
narrative unity and complexity.

It is hard, of course, to draw any fixed line between narrative and
dramatic modes, especially in an age like the present where novelists
attempt to erase from their novels any hint of their own presence—
to "render" rather than to "tell"—and where dramatists like Brecht
attempt to create a narrative, as opposed to a dramatic, theater. But
if we accept Kellogg and Scholes's basic definition that a narrative is a
"literary work . . . distinguished by two characteristics: the presence
of a story and the storyteller" as contrasted with drama, which is "a
story without a storyteller [in which] characters act out directly what
Aristotle called an 'imitation' of such actions as we find in life,"
certain differences in the effects of the two modes become immediately clear.[26]

First, because of this basic distinction between the tale told and
the drama enacted, the quality of imaginative response demanded by
narrative and by drama is inevitably different: in narrative, the
audience must "body forth" the forms of characters and settings; in

drama, such embodying is done for the audience, but the audience must itself seek the meanings, relationships, and connections provided in narrative by the narrator. Thus Shakespeare's introduction of narrative devices and figures into his Romances creates a complex, often tension-filled imaginative experience for the audience. Second, simply because it has a narrator, a narrative can cover a much longer period of time, can include a greater number and variety of events, and can move freely in space and time, as Aristotle noted.[27] In a narrative, in other words, because there is both a tale and a teller of the tale, the very shape of the work is automatically affected. Gerald Else, expanding on Aristotle's comment, explains that "to the narrator, just because he is a narrator, all events lie open and immediately accessible: they are all equally present at the time they are related. If in telling a story I jump back ten years, the time jumps with me; the event I am now narrating is just as much present to me and my auditors as the other one . . . was a moment ago. Narrative is a magic carpet which can transport us anywhere in the twinkling of an eye and then take up its course" (*Aristotle's Poetics*, p. 609). Drama, in contrast, is a story told through action and dialogue and is, by Aristotle's definition, restricted to forward-moving, seemingly continuous action. Thus, "it is inherent in the *idea* of the drama as a continuous action going on at a certain place and enacted by a given set of people" (Else, p. 609) that the time perspective is single and that the number of events is more limited than in narrative.

The "sovereign freedom" of the narrative (Else, p. 610) to move freely in time and space, to manipulate characters and events at will —expanding, contracting, dismissing with a word—Shakespeare brings to *The Winter's Tale* first through its narrator-chorus, Father Time, whose thoughts can "slide / O'er sixteen years, and leave the growth untried / Of that wide gap," who speaks of "my tale," "my scene"; who transforms dramatized action of the play to narrative by

85

referring to earlier dramatized events as if they had been "told" to us by him: "Remember well / I mention'd a son o' th' king's," he says, recalling the dramatized discussion of Florizel in 1.2. Later, in the narrated recognition scene (5.2), narrative freedom again obtains. The effect of this scene is essentially narrative: the three gentlemen are not characterized, there is no conflict among them, no sense of action moving forward. Their theme, like that of narrative in general, is the past,[28] and they move freely through past time, touching now on the immediately witnessed recognition scene, now on the abandonment of Perdita sixteen years before, now on Leontes' reunion with Polixenes, now on Antigonus's long-ago fate in Bohemia. Their references to the incredibility of the tales they relate reduce the play as a whole to a "winter's tale" and condition our response to the action we have seen, and to that which will come. The play, then, is like a tale, a tale which comes vividly to life only to be "staled" or gently mocked by narrator figures. Like narrative, it covers a long period of time and includes a long succession of wonderful events.

In *Cymbeline,* no narrator as such appears and there is no scene which is entirely "narrative,"—but narrative devices abound, and are used to lend a narrative freedom to the incredibly complex plot. The opening scene includes long reports of the life histories of various characters: Posthumus's life story is rehearsed, as is the story of the stealing of the young princes some twenty years earlier. Throughout the play, extradramatic monologues continue the narrative manner established by this opening scene, as they summarize the action, provide links between dramatized scenes, connect disparate plot threads, or fill in background information. Such soliloquies as Pisanio's

> I heard no letter from my master since
> I wrote him Imogen was slain. 'Tis strange!

> Nor hear I from my mistress, who did promise
> To yield me often tidings. Neither know I
> What is betid to Cloten; but remain
> Perplex'd in all.   (4.3.36ff)

give to the plot of *Cymbeline* a narrative freedom comparable to that we find in *The Winter's Tale*. Once the dramatist allows a character temporarily to assume a narrator role (as does Belarius when he fills in the twenty-year gap in the history of the lost princes) the drama can move easily in the direction of narrative. It can include numerous plot threads, complex patterns of interweaving, countless digressions, great freedom in the handling of time, because, as in narrative, much can be explained or related. This, of course, is what happens in *Cymbeline*, as one character after another takes on a narrative function. Again, the sense of time passing, of wonderful events and far wanderings, is dominant.

In *The Tempest*, Prospero's function as narrator is all-important. As in much good narrative, his function varies from scene to scene: he comments, he describes, he reminds us of simultaneous plot threads, or he simply summarizes undramatized action. At first, he is narrator-as-expositor, rehearsing to Miranda, to Ariel, and to Caliban their earlier histories. When Ferdinand is led on stage, Prospero plays a double role, first, as actor in the dramatic situation (a false role which he puts on in order to intensify the attraction between Miranda and Ferdinand) and, second, in his asides, as narrator-as-commentator. In the Harpy scene, he resumes his role of narrator and commentator and takes on the further role of plot-connector: watching the nobles below him, he reminds us of what Ferdinand and Miranda are at the moment doing elsewhere on the island. Later, his sudden recollection of Caliban's conspiracy during the wedding masque once again narratively connects two plots, creating for us the sense that disparate actions are occurring in the play simultaneously. And, as *The Tempest* reaches its end, Prospero's role of narrator-commentator becomes heavily elaborated. In earlier scenes, his commentary is limited to brief asides which tell us what is happening onstage ("At the first sight / They have chang'd eyes") or which evaluate the action for us ("It goes on, I see, / As my soul prompts it"); but in the later scenes, Prospero's explanations and descriptions are more important than the actions they describe. His famous *tirade* on the fading of the masque and his description of the awakening of the nobles from their state of madness

> The charm dissolves apace;
> And as the morning steals upon the night,
> Melting the darkness, so their rising senses
> Begin to chase the ignorant fumes that mantle
> Their clearer reason . . .   (Ll. 64–68)

are so powerful as narrative commentaries that the accompanying stage actions seem to be merely illustrative gestures—ballet movements—to illustrate the poetry. During much of this play, and especially at moments like this, Prospero-as-*dramatis-persona* and Prospero-as-stage-manager are subordinated to Prospero-the-narrator, and *The Tempest* takes on the characteristics of a powerful first-person narrative.

One major reason that the surface strategies of the three Romances seem so unlike each other is that the proportions of drama and narrative in *Cymbeline, The Winter's Tale,* and *The Tempest* vary widely, as Shakespeare chooses to seek dramatic emphasis here or narrative complexity there. *Cymbeline,* for instance, is built much like a Greek Romance, with multiple story lines, tales-within-tales, separate tracings of the adventures of the young lovers, pseudohistorical background, complex denouement; its structure, then, is essentially narrative.[29] Yet *Cymbeline* has no single "narrator"; this role is shared by a number of characters in turn. *The Winter's Tale*, in contrast, makes important use of its narrator figure: Father Time's comments not only provide narrative continuity, but also shape our reactions to "the Leontes-story," just as the three narrators in 5.2 tell important parts of the story and influence our feelings about the tale as a whole. But this play, built on a Renaissance version of Greek Romance, selects two large sections of the romance to dramatize, superficially observing, within these dramatized segments, the normal design of Shakespearean drama; narrative structure and manner are reserved for the extradramatic scenes which surround and link the dramatic actions. And in *The Tempest*, all is dramatized and all is "told." The action does not stop while a narrator tells us what is happening or what we are to think; even the long narrations making up most of act 1, scene 2—in context, much like the chorus of *The Winter's Tale*, or like the monologue of Belarius in *Cymbeline*—are made semidramatic through Prospero's chidings of Miranda to pay attention and through the interplay between the angry Prospero and the rebellious Ariel and Caliban. Yet, in *The Tempest*, drama and narrative blend so subtly that we are at once, through Prospero, both shown and told the story.

The more one contemplates the blending of narrative and drama in *The Tempest*, the more impressed one is with Shakespeare's absolute mastery of artistic form in this play and the more one realizes the demands made by this play on the imaginative response of the audience. In the Harpy scene, for instance (3.3), narrative and drama continually play against each other, often occurring simultaneously, and demanding from the audience a multitude of responses, some mutually contradictory. The scene begins with "drama" as the Court Party enters, exhausted:

GONZALO: By'r Lakin, I can go no further, sir!
My old bones ache . . .
ALONSO: Old lord, I cannot blame thee,
Who am myself attach'd with weariness
To th' dulling of my spirits. Sit down and rest.

(Ll. 1–6)

These seem to us real people—tired, discouraged, depressed:

ALONSO: He is drown'd
Whom thus we stray to find; and the sea mocks
Our frustrate search on land. Well, let him go.

(Ll. 8–10)

With the asides of Sebastian and Antonio (Ll. 11–16) as the villains plot against the discouraged old men, a new note enters, a modulation, through "asides," from the objective drama which opens the scene toward the narrative/spectacle which suddenly intrudes. Prospero enters, on the top, "invisible," to the sound of "strange and solemn music." What follows is a blend of highly theatrical spectacle, objective drama, and narrative. Most obtrusive is the spectacle: a banquet which appears, and later disappears "with a quaint device," strange music, sounds of thunder, monstrous creatures who dance and "mock and mow." But objective drama continues simultaneously as the Court Party responds to the scene "naturalistically" and characteristically: to Sebastian, the appearance of the banquet proves that fantasy-creations are indeed true; to Gonzalo, the actions of the spirits call forth philosophic comments. The appearance of the Harpy is a signal for all to draw their swords, just as the banquet is a reminder of their hunger. The words of the Harpy produce in Alonso very "natural" reactions: first, horror and guilt for his past actions;

then, recognition that he (like Leontes in *The Winter's Tale*) was, through his own actions, responsible for the death of his son; and, finally, despair, and the decision to drown himself and lie bedded in the ooze with Ferdinand. The dramatized response of the Court Party is a constant in this scene, and the scene ends, as it begins, with objective drama as Alonso sets out once again on a journey.

Yet over the major part of the scene looms the figure of Prospero—invisible to the other characters, but constantly drawing our attention away from them and the spectacle being presented to them. There he stands, knowing all and controlling all. To Gonzalo's reflections on the gentleness of the island spirits as compared with humans, Prospero comments:

> Honest lord,
> Thou has said well; for some of you there present
> Are worse than devils.   (Ll. 34–36)

This single aside to the audience at once validates Gonzalo's statement, shows us the extent of Prospero's knowledge of the characters, and reduces the scene being played at his feet to a puppet show. Again, when Alonso notes the "excellent dumb discourse" of the spirits, Prospero's aside—"Praise in departing"—reminds us that he knows more than the other characters—more, indeed, than we.

As Ariel in the guise of a Harpy chastises the three men of sin, Prospero watches from above approvingly, and departs in order to take part in another plot line of his story after giving an aside to the audience, a final narrator statement to remind us that it is indeed his "play" that we are watching—that in effect he wrote the words for Ariel-as-Harpy to say:

> Bravely the figure of this harpy hast thou
> Perform'd, my Ariel; a grace it had, devouring.

> Of my instruction hast thou nothing bated
> In what thou hadst to say.
>
> .   .   .   .
>
> They now are in my pow'r;
> And in these fits I leave them, while I visit
> Young Ferdinand, whom they suppose is drown'd,
> And his and mine lov'd darling. (Ll. 83–93)

Mimetic drama, interrupted by supernatural spectacle, all under the general control of narrative—a strange blend, but one characteristic of *The Tempest* and comparable in effect only to certain scenes in Shakespeare's other Romances—and to Greek Romance narratives. In Greek Romance, drama is transferred to novel form; both ancient critics and the writers of Greek Romances recognize the literary/dramatic backgrounds and general effect of the Greek Romances by calling them "dramatic narratives" or even sometimes "dramas." In them, as in *The Tempest*, we are caught in the tension between dramatic, implausible, theatrical action, on the one hand, and omniscient narration on the other. For the reader, nothing is "expected," since sudden reversals and intrusions from the unknown keep us always on edge; for the narrator, all is known, and all will be revealed when the narrator chooses. Hence the tension. The dual nature of Greek Romance as "historiography" and "drama" has been discussed fully by Ben Edwin Perry,[30] and need not be examined here, but what has not been noted is that Shakespeare, primarily through the intimate blending of narrative and drama, has captured, especially in *The Tempest*, the effect of Greek Romance. It is as if Shakespeare, in his Romances, is reversing the process of Heliodorous or Chariton: they turn serious drama, with its conflicts and trial scenes and recognitions and set dialogues, into "dramatic narrative"; Shakespeare takes the prose-romance form and transfers it to the stage, producing a kind of narrative drama—a drama which, as A. D. Nuttall notes, offers us "a sense of a shimmering multiplicity of levels."[31]

A narrative/dramatic mode is essential in conveying the shape and tone of romance onstage. If a romance story is turned into "real" drama, complete with midplay climactic complications and a decisive turning point action, with dramatic forward movement from expectation to fulfillment, with presentation solely in the objective mode of action and dramatic dialogue, the romance quality is inevitably distorted. The sense of inevitability and of immediateness which drama seeks is inimical to romance. Hence, even though many of Shakespeare's plays are romance-based,[32] including in them a large share of inherently incredible events and a large number of extradramatic devices which open the story out to the audience in a manner reminiscent of narrative, Shakespeare, by giving his more "dramatically structured" plays a dramatic shape and intensity, creates dramas of immediacy and inevitability far removed from their romance origins. In his last plays, however, he gives us "romance" as such. He no longer makes use of his earlier methods of transforming narrative into drama; rather, he breaks his normal dramaturgical patterns; he emphasizes the story element, the surprises, the whimsicality of action, the "once upon a time" quality of his tale; and he introduces author surrogates to mediate between action and audience. This mixed, seminarrative mode in *Cymbeline*, *The Winter's Tale*, and *The Tempest* enables Shakespeare to tell a Romance story in such a way that the quality and tone of romance are more or less unaltered in their transferal to the stage.

When, in the Romances, Shakespeare blends tragic and comic views, when he mixes presentational and representational styles, when he mingles narrative with drama, he creates a new kind of Shakespearean drama—a kind which is throughout an extension of his

93

earlier work. To study this "kind" of drama and to try to find answers to questions raised in this and earlier chapters will be the purpose of the following chapters. For the moment I would like to return to the important essay by Clifford Leech to which I referred above (p. 69). Professor Leech recognizes that the structure of the last plays is different from that of Shakespeare's other plays and he senses a disturbance of some kind within that structure. His conclusion is that Shakespeare had begun to view experience as "cyclic," and that each of the last plays represents a more or less successful attempt to impose a "crisis" action on the cyclic experience. Only *The Winter's Tale*, he argues, is a successful fusion of crisis and cycle; both *Cymbeline* and *The Tempest* suffer from Shakespeare's inability to force cyclic experience into crisis form.

In the light of what we have seen of the dramatic strategy of the last plays, I would reject this picture of a Shakespeare struggling unsuccessfully to incorporate a new vision in a now uncongenial dramatic form, and would suggest instead that, structurally, the plays are experimental blends of narrative and dramatic modes. The effect of the experiment is reasonably apparent: Shakespeare has created, in his last plays, a kind of dramatic form—and, consequently, a kind of dramatic experience—different from his other creations, not as uniformly dramatic, but richly complex. In the last plays, themes that are always a part of the Shakespearean world are grown so "wonderful" that they can be expressed only by a ballad-maker who has learned that life is "like an old tale still." And the structure of the plays, which makes them as much like tales as like drama, helps us to experience—rather than merely to become intellectually aware of —the wonder and complexity of story, of drama, and of life.

CHAPTER IV

The Romances as Open Form Drama

I have thus far traced three strands in the dramaturgical pattern of the Romances. "The hour's now come," as Prospero would put it, to examine the pattern woven by these strands. Given the conflation of tragedy and comedy, of presentational and representational styles, of narrative and dramatic modes, what shall we make of these plays as dramatic constructs?

Let us begin by looking at a drama in which the pattern of the Romances appears clearly and unambiguously. This play, *Pericles, Prince of Tyre*,[1] precedes *Cymbeline, The Winter's Tale,* and *The Tempest* and obviously influenced Shakespeare deeply, no matter how much of a hand he had in its shaping or its writing. *Pericles* is unlike the Romances which we are studying in that it does not retell an earlier Shakespearean fable and in that it emphasizes quest and Job-like suffering in a way foreign to the other Romances. It differs from them, again, in the relation it sets up with the audience; we are not mystified or misled, but are let into all the secrets: only briefly do we think that Thaisa is dead, and never do we believe with Pericles that his daughter is forever lost to him. Yet in many respects—formal and thematic—*Pericles* is to the other Romances as a musical theme is to its variations. *Pericles* states in bold, clear, simple tones the rhythms and many of the motifs that will be varied most wonderfully in *Cymbeline, The Winter's Tale,* and *The Tempest.*

In *Pericles* comedy and tragedy are starkly juxtaposed, with scenes of dance, lovemaking, fatherly scheming, and joyful union followed swiftly by the heart sorrow of Thaisa's death and sea burial;

representational style repeatedly gives way to obtrusive presentations: dumb shows, processions, supernatural visions; dramatic form is again and again destroyed as Gower tells and shows his musty tale, leading us through one incredible adventure after another until climax and denouement coincide in final reunions. Formally, the pattern of *Pericles*—a pattern characterized by chaotic dramatic rhythms, by repeated breaking of ongoing generic and stylistic forms, and by continual narrative interruptions of the dramatic flow—recurs variously in each of our three Romances, with Shakespeare in each one taking the basic formal pattern of *Pericles* and reworking it to make three separate, though related, dramatic statements. Thematic motifs, introduced in *Pericles*, also recur in the Romances. The power of the father-daughter relationship, the simultaneous cruelty and kindness of Nature, chastity as a virtue related to fruitful union and opposed to the horrors of lust, supernatural forces shaping the action, magic restorations of life, unbelievable reunions—these themes, central to *Pericles*, are picked up and varied, sometimes as counterpoint, sometimes as central melody, in each of our three Romances.

When we look at the blendings of formal patterns and thematic motifs in *Pericles* and the later Romances, we find plays that are in many ways unique: fairy tale stories stripped of oversentimentality by sharply crafted dramaturgy. Yet if we look at the formal patterns alone, we find not unique plays, but examples of a special dramatic kind with a long and venerable history. This "kind," which includes such diverse examples as Aristophanic comedy, Renaissance masques, *The Knight of the Burning Pestle*, and Brechtian epic dramas, shares a common avoidance of those traditional dramatic formal controls which one associates with Aristotelian or "mimetic" drama. Numerous critics have sought to capture the essence of this non-Aristotelian drama which, often perversely, seems to break through the generic, stylistic, and mimetic forms which shape the majority of stage plays,

great and mediocre alike.[2] In the following discussion I attempt my
own definition of this elusive dramatic kind in the hope that a more
systematic study of what I will call "open form drama"[3] will help
us put Shakespeare's Romances in a larger dramatic perspective (thus
making sense of the strands of the dramaturgical patterns we have
already traced) and will perhaps open up new ways of approaching
other difficult dramas within this same structural mold.

Any study of dramatic form must begin with the recognition that
"form" in the temporal arts is no tangible, visual entity; thus, concepts like Heinrich Wölfflin's painterly/linear, plane/recession, or
closed form/open form distinctions, so useful in talking about form
in the plastic arts, must be used with incredible care when one discusses literary, dramatic, or musical forms.[4] Wölfflin, for example, in
describing painting, sculpture, and architecture, can talk meaningfully about "symmetry about a central axis" or about the relationship
of given elements to the work's "frame." In the temporal arts, no
fixed visual or tangible form exists; the work moves through time,
and is indeed created (for the auditor/spectator) *in* time. Thus, to
apply meaningful distinctions to the various forms of a temporal art,
one must begin with a definition of form which takes into account
its basic temporal dimension.

Such a definition one finds in Kenneth Burke's view of literary
form as a curve—a temporal curve that traces audience response from
initial expectation to intermediate frustration to final satisfaction.
Burke has analyzed how such a curve is created in literary works,
through progressive forms (syllogistic and qualitative), through conventional forms (often including the generic), and through repetitive
and minor forms.[5] Leonard Meyer has demonstrated brilliantly the
comparable methods of achieving such form in music.[6] In both
literature and music, "notes" are initially struck which bring into

existence the first part of a formal pattern; our attention is drawn to the development of this pattern: situations demand to be overcome, imbalances righted, dissonant chords resolved. As we move from "once upon a time" to "and they lived happily ever after," we live within the frame of the Burkeian curve, detached from the unpatterned language or sound flow surrounding us, caught up in a developing, shaping form.[7]

It is my suggestion that literary works which follow this curve—which are based upon syllogistic or qualitative progression, which work within generic conventions, which make use of repetitive and incidental forms to give a sense of unity, of coherence, of wholeness to the work and to the experience of responding to the work—are comparable to Wölfflin's "closed form" paintings (self-consistent works which depend on symmetry, enclosed patterns, a seemingly deliberate relationship to the lines and angles that "frame" the work and separate it from the world around it). "Open form" literary works, then, are those which avoid this Burkeian curve. Such works do not follow syllogistic or qualitative progressions (progressions in which "one incident in the plot" prepares us for some incident to follow logically, or in which "we are put into a state of mind in which another state of mind can logically follow"—in which, in other words, the premises stated or the problems raised in the initial situation are decisively resolved in the final action);[8] they, instead, avoid any obvious line of determined action, and are characterized by an undercutting of the balance, shape, symmetry of the closed-form work by a seeming refusal to allow one incident to demand a particular succeeding incident. Instead of significant use of repetitive devices (successions of "images, each . . . regiving the same lyric mood; a character repeating his identity . . . under changing situations; the sustaining of an attitude, as in satire; the rhythmic regularity of blank verse"—Burke, p. 125), the normal repetitive forms are interrupted, with rhythmical and metrical patterns broken and characters complex or inconsistent. The tone or mood of the piece avoids consistency and appears flexible and sometimes multiple, uncertain, or jarringly changeable.

Open form drama, specifically, is that drama in which cause-and-effect patterns are broken, generic conventions abandoned (and with them the easily established point of view, of attitude, that observance of generic conventions make possible), and the dramatic illusion repeatedly broken through narrative intrusion, spectacle, and other sudden disturbances of the aesthetic distance. The resulting casual relationship with the audience gives a sense of unintentionality, of Wölfflin's "adventitiousness,"[9] of refusal to stay within the created art world, which seems to break all dramatic patterns and which creates a startlingly non-Aristotelian dramatic form.

Open form dramas—as here defined—have, as I noted above, appeared sporadically in the history of theater. Aristophanic comedy, for instance, though in some ways bounded by comic form, breaks syllogistic expectation patterns with its seemingly random patterning of episodes growing out of the early *agon;* it sets up a casual, direct relationship with the audience by directing comments (often scathing attacks) to individual members of the audience and by including a choral *parabasis* to defend the author's own dramatic works or his personal beliefs. Elizabethan and Jacobean masques, too, generally ignore syllogistic dramatic progression in favor of narrative presentation and spectacle, and include the audience in the performance, both through the close relation between audience and masque presenter and through the mingling of audience and actors in a final dance. Modern epic and theatricalist theater deliberately breaks the normal patterns which shape closed form drama by moving beyond tragedy and comedy, by interspersing presentation with mimesis, and by using narrative devices freely.[10]

99

These examples of the large body of drama which I am calling "open form" seem various, but they are alike in aiming not at aesthetic satisfaction (the aim, according to Richard Schechner, of "mimetic" drama) but rather at theatrical experience which breaks through the aesthetic, deliberately destroying dramatic coherence and consistency in order to waken us to new insights or to disturbing truths, or to provide us with an experience sharply different from the experience of watching closed form drama. Northrop Frye makes this distinction between closed and open form in his discussion of modern arts, though he does not use the open-vs.-closed terminology.[11] For Frye, classical art and music seek perfection of form; "modern" arts tend "to prefer the imperfect work engaged in history to the perfected masterpiece that pulls away from time" (p. 71). As we see in the following passage, Frye's definition of form is Burkeian, and his distinction between classic and modern art is suggestively parallel to that distinction I am suggesting between closed and open form drama:

> Classical music, up to quite recent times has been intensely teleological: in symphonies from Haydn to Brahms we feel strongly how the end of a movement is implied in the beginning, and how we are led towards it step by step. In much contemporary music . . . the emphasis is on the immediate sense impression of sound: the music is not going anywhere . . . The ear is not thrown forward into the future, to hear a theme being worked out or a discord resolved; it is kept sternly in the present moment. This conception of the unit of experience as a thing in itself is of course an intensely impersonal attitude to art: the writer (and similarly with the other arts) is doing all he can to avoid the sense of impressing himself on his reader by suggesting meaning or form or purpose beyond what is presented. In

this conception of *chosisme*, as it is sometimes called, it is not simply continuity, but significance or meaning itself, which has been handed over to the reader. (Pp. 72–73)

The curve of expectation is broken, the senses are focused on the present, the making of a consistent, meaningful artwork is put largely in the hands of the audience: an interesting definition of "modern" arts of all kinds, and of the structure of open form drama of all periods.

To see Shakespeare's Romances as open form drama is in many ways helpful. First, as I mentioned above, by linking the Romances to this larger body of drama, we offer a new context in which to set and to examine the plays. Once we recognize the existence of a kind of drama that deliberately goes against "standard" dramaturgical practices, we can look more clear-sightedly at Shakespeare's own creations in this form. His breaking of forms becomes a positive statement to be examined in a larger historical frame, and abstract pronouncements about Shakespeare's experimentation in his Romances can become properly focused.

In this context, we can see, for example, that in the Romances, expectation patterns (generic, stylistic, tonal) are not so much ignored as they are deliberately flouted. Tragic patterns collide with comic devices; presentational techniques mock representational style; narrative intrudes into mimetic action. Interestingly, the patterns which conflict with each other, each bringing its own set of expectations, are Shakespearean patterns. The representational style of these plays is a style Shakespeare himself had developed, just as the presentational elements which interrupt it are reminiscent of Shakespeare's own early work. The dramatic form which is broken is Shakespeare's own form, nowhere more perfectly embodied than in

Shakespeare's plays. And his use of fables he had earlier treated in comedy and tragedy seems to indicate his awareness that it is his own comic or tragic world which is being thrown into a new perspective by the confrontation with its opposite. In other words, his "experimentation" consists in using his own formal patterns in a new way—a way that suggests, first, complete confidence in his ability to control his audience's response, and, second, a magnificent freedom. Only a dramatist who had thoroughly mastered his medium could so detach himself from the forms that they no longer control the shape of the art object. Shakespeare, in the Romances, controls the forms throughout, playing them one against the other with seeming detachment and, one suspects, with amusement.

Further, the open form label helps us to make crucial dramaturgical distinctions between Shakespeare's Romances and his earlier closed form plays—distinctions which are not at first sight obvious. The distinctions are hidden, first, by the fact that almost all of Shakespeare's plays tend toward openness of form. All include a basic narrative line along which the semiautonomous scenes are strung;[12] all occasionally break the dramatic illusion with devices which overstep the aesthetic frame and intrude into the spectator's "real" world; all stand ready to shift our perspective at any moment from compassion to mirth, to change the action context from the tragic to the comic, from the romantic to the ironic. But—and here is where the distinction appears—Shakespearean drama in general includes what we might call "strong closing devices": emotionally heightened midplay action which concentrates and focuses the work; a consistent aesthetic surface which the occasional extradramatic monologue disturbs but little; general dependence on the formal restraints of conventional generic forms: a persistent and skillful use of repetitive forms (in stage imagery, character development, arrangement of situations, recurring metaphors) to give a sense of unity and self-containedness to the play. In Shakespeare's Romances, in contrast, the normal Shakespearean methods of achieving essentially closed form drama are avoided, and the plays, as a consequence, have the appearance of casualness, of deliberate artlessness, of "adventitiousness," which we associate with open form art in general.

To make this distinction more obvious, let us again look briefly at *The Tempest*, the one Romance that is superficially "closed," but which, of all the Romances, is actually most complex in its use of open form dramaturgy. Within any individual scene in *The Tempest*, for instance, situations begin as closed form actions: two villains prepare to murder a king, or two drunken castaways conspire with a native monster to find and destroy the master of the island; expectations begin to develop, we sense a situation growing, logically and dramatically, to some kind of climax: then suddenly Prospero as magician intervenes, and closed form drama becomes open. Using sleep, music, and magic as his means, Prospero destroys the normal action bases, and the characters cease to be rational subjects, whose actions we can anticipate, and become passive objects, who sleep, wake, become paralyzed, or follow invisible spirits at the will of the magician-hero.[13]

In larger structure, too, *The Tempest* is complex, built on a subtle combination of open and closed effects, so handled that we are never quite sure whether the frame play—the opening and closing scenes— is open background—" a primary level of openness"—or a closed frame; whether the enclosed play is majestic vision or closed, concrete action. For Erika Flamm, the first and last scenes of the play are open, leading the eye and the mind away from the action on the island, encouraging us to feel that the dramatized action is but a small piece of a much larger story. The fact that the region referred to in these frame scenes (that "region where the antecedent action takes place, whence all the dramatic figures have come and where they will once again return") is "not something identical to reality beyond the work of art," that it "belongs to the fictive, aesthetically shaped realm of the drama itself," and that it is "not dramatized, but extends before and behind the dramatized scenes," demonstrates in one more instance, she suggests, "the openness of *The Tempest*."[14] For Robert Nelson, too, the first and last scenes of *The Tempest* act as a frame for an enclosed play.[15] "The peripheral moments" of the drama, he says, "are like the frames of many plays within plays" in Shakespearean drama. And in many ways "the portion contained within these frames itself reminds us of a play: the isle is the stage; Ariel, Caliban, Miranda, and the rescued passengers the actors; Prospero that man of the theater we have recognized Shakespeare himself to have been: playwright, actor, director" (Nelson, p. 30). Yet for Nelson, the first and last scenes are mimetic, made up of realistic moments of shipwreck and renunciation, enclosing a "majestic vision" which is the central action of the play.

However we choose to view the "plays" presented in *The Tempest*, the suggestion that the action on the island is a play-within-a-play raises the intriguing possibility that, in *The Tempest* (and perhaps in *Cymbeline* and *The Winter's Tale* as well) Shakespeare has somehow turned us into the Theseus and Hippolyta-like audience of *A Midsummer Night's Dream*—that is, instead of providing actor-spectators to watch Prospero's "play," he has given the audience that role; he has caught us up in a system composed of open drama plus audience—a system which the "Pyramus and Thisbe" scene presents in entirety onstage, but which, in the last plays, takes in the auditorium as well. By breaking down the customary expectation patterns in the Romances, Shakespeare places us not, as in normal Shakespearean drama, in a position of dramatic expectancy about what will happen, but in the position of innocent, wondering auditors. By manipulating audience-stage involvement and detachment, he catches

the audience up in the play, making of the stage-audience relationship
a kind of closed play of more significance than the admittedly fraudulent make-believe play going on onstage. He thus makes the
audience active participants in the creation of the aesthetic experience
and shifts the effect from the single, unified, coherent, to the complex, diverse, multiple.

As David Young points out, "Any drama can be described as a set
of experiences in two distinct ways. On the one hand it is an account
of the experience undergone by a group of fictitious characters and
held in common by them. In addition, however, as played before an
audience, it is also an experience undergone by a group of real
characters, as witnesses, and undergone by them."[16] In the Romances,
because of the open form dramaturgy, the experience undergone
by the audience is, as I suggested, necessarily complex and diverse.
Note how, for instance within almost any given scene of these plays,
the dramaturgy makes it almost impossible for the audience to respond simply—or even coherently. For example, in *The Tempest* in
act 3, scene 3—the scene examined in detail in chapter 3—because the
action shifts rapidly from mimetic drama to a confluence of spectacle,
drama, and narrative in which our senses are flooded ("solemn and
strange music," "strange shapes" which dance and gesture to the king,
Prospero "on top," an amazed and defiant Court Party), our reactions
are necessarily complex. The mode is neither comic nor tragic; the
mixture of mimetic drama and spectacle makes our "distance" from
the action uncertain; and Prospero's reminders that he has planned the
spectacle and its effect on the Court Party, while we ourselves have
no idea what to expect, creates further tension. The tension breaks
slightly during those moments in which Prospero comments wryly and
amusingly, or in which the Court Party responds awkwardly or
angrily to the spectacles, but the tension builds again and again as we
are, for example, first distanced by the sudden appearance of the

Harpy and the spectacle of the disappearing banquet, then suddenly engaged by the power of the Harpy's speech and its effect on the men. As the speech ends, with its threats of "lingering perdition" and its urging of "heart's sorrow / And a clear life ensuing," we seem momentarily caught up in representational Shakespearean drama. The powerful speech of chastisement demands an equally powerful speech of repentance and despair—and the speech, and a dramatic flight from the stage, do occur. But this is open form drama: thus, the Harpy's speech and Alonso's response to it, instead of occurring as an extended dramatic moment to which we can give an extended response, are sharply separated, first by another spectacle of strange shapes, then by a long narrative speech from Prospero. Because of the form of the scene, our experience, in spite of our awareness of Prospero's magic power, is not that of being placed "above the fluctuations of belief and disbelief that swirl around the characters" (as David Young would have it)[17] but is, instead, one of dislocation and amazement.

Such an effect is in sharp contrast to that created by earlier Shakespearean drama, even that drama which has much in common with the Romances. In *Comedy of Errors* and in *Twelfth Night*, for example—plays which share with the Romances a source in Greek Romance—our experience of the plays differs from our response to the Romances. Jackson I. Cope's comment (based on Jean Rousset's study of French baroque)[18] that "in Shakespeare's *Comedy of Errors* . . . waking life and dream illusions become so interwoven that Rousset can remark, 'il semble qu'on y voie naître le theatre sous la forme du songe éveillé' " is not really valid. It is true that for some of the characters in *Comedy of Errors* (as later for Sebastian in *Twelfth Night*), "life" does indeed seem a dream or a magic enchantment. To those characters, because there are certain facts that they do not know, waking laws of cause and effect, of normal space and time, seem in abeyance, and they ask, with other persons of M. Rousset's baroque, "Rêve-je ou si je veille?"

But for the audience, no such confusions exist. *Comedy of Errors* does offer us one surprise in the emergence of the mother as abbess—but, with this one exception, in *Comedy of Errors*, as in *Twelfth Night*, Shakespeare keeps us carefully informed of the "truth" so that we can enjoy the characters' bewilderment; we are, in general, kept within the comic genre, shielded from suffering and given a mirth-provoking world of mistaken identities and comic recognitions. Thus, although the frame story of *Comedy of Errors* approaches open form dramaturgy, this play, like *Twelfth Night*, is essentially closed in form, and our response to both of these earlier Greek Romance plays is less complex, less various, than our response to the Romances. For not until the writing of *Cymbeline*, *The Winter's Tale*, and *The Tempest* do we find Shakespeare consistently reaching out to take the audience into a world where "waking life and dream illusions" are truly interwoven—where, because of the dramaturgy of the plays, we, like the characters, experience bewilderment and uncertainty in the face of the unstable, true/false world of Romance.

The earlier tragicomedies, too, though reminiscent of the Romances in their use of the tragicomic genre, are very unlike them in effect. *Troilus and Cressida*, *Measure for Measure*, and *All's Well That Ends Well* are closed form dramas in which the action centers on a problem to be solved or a situation to be coped with. The audience is kept carefully informed of necessary facts, and kept carefully within the Antinomy of Distance; the plots follow unerring syllogistic progressions. Human reason is exalted; cleverness in the manipulation of others and clear-sightedness about human frailty are shown to be the prerequisites for success in the closed tragicomic world. The sense of human control of human destiny is conveyed through the syllogistically constructed action; the awareness of prob-

lems solved or situations coped with grows out of the changed con-
figuration at the end of the play: because of what has happened in
the play, the characters at the end stand in a new relationship to each
other and to their world. We can talk meaningfully about the central
conflict in each play and can discuss the working out of the problems
in relation to the characters and their character traits.

If we approach the Romances—open form tragicomedies—in this
way, we misread the plays. Consider, for example, Jan Kott's analysis
of *The Tempest*. Although Kott points out many things that are true
about the play, he reads the play as closed form drama, as a serious
action unfolding and working itself out to a resolution. Thus, in attempting to isolate the dramatic conflict, the "problem" with which
the play deals, he sees the play as "a great Renaissance tragedy of
lost illusions."[19] Yet this is a very partial view of this play. For it is
not just bad productions of *The Tempest* which keep its essential
bitterness from our awareness, as Kott claims; it is, rather, the
dramaturgy itself which forbids us to take this play world so seriously
that we see Prospero and Caliban as tragic or the action as representing the tragically violent history of the world.

Unlike the earlier tragicomedies, the Romances do not focus on
a problem or a central conflict or idea; they are instead circularly
open, with the entire movement of each play in the direction of a
return to original happiness—not to a new happiness better than that
which opened the play (as in most of the comedies), but instead to
a happiness approximating that known at an earlier time. Though
time and death take their toll in the Romances, the action tends
always toward restoration: the plays return wives to husbands, children to fathers, dukes to their dukedoms. Instead of problem-centered
action which emphasizes the power of human reason, these plays give
us stories in which illusions about human reason are overthrown, as
neither cleverness, intellect, nor clear-sightedness avail to give the

characters control over their lives. Except for Prospero-as-magician, these characters cannot control worlds which are in the grip of chance, magic, or a god on a golden eagle; nor can they control themselves, for they are as subject to attack from the irrational forces within as they are to blows struck from the mysterious world surrounding them.

Pirandello, in describing his antirationalist theater, said that his task was to tear down the white columns which the Greeks had erected over the dark abyss.[20] There is something of this in what Shakespeare has done in his last plays, where human reason and human cleverness (unless assisted by magic) are powerless in the face of the irrational; human goodness is a sometime thing, set upon by bestiality without and within; earthquake passions destroy the human constructs of tradition, rationality, and custom, unless an equally mysterious force—magic, the supernatural, a chance emotion—intervenes. Crucial to this "tearing down" is the open form dramaturgy, which separates action from sequential action, action from acting character—and which allows Shakespeare to present isolated phenomena of human experience detached from the patterns which are normally imposed upon them by closed form drama.

If we overlook the non-Aristotelian form of these plays and insist on seeing them as peculiar attempts to create "normal" Shakespearean drama, we will tend, as I noted above, to misread these plays; further, we may allow our attempts to establish norms of Shakespearean dramaturgy to be thwarted by the refusal of the Romances to conform to these norms; worse yet, we will respond unfavorably to presentations of the Romances which take into account their differences from more "typical" Shakespeare. Interrupted actions, varying aesthetic distance, spectacle, narrative fragments, lyric poetry, once-upon-a-time story: this is the very stuff of Shakespeare's open form drama; and it is to this, and to the total experience created by this drama, that we must look for the meaning that these plays offer. Potentially sentimental fairy tales, the sentiment stripped away by the open form dramaturgy; drama and narrative so conjoined that the powers of both forms rise to rich and strange heights—partial descriptions of Shakespeare's Romances: Shakespeare "with a difference." Only after we have seen this difference in form can we begin even tentatively to explore the meanings contingent on the forms.

CHAPTER V

Form and Meaning: Some Implications

"Works of art are not mirrors, but they share with mirrors that elusive
magic of transformation which is so hard to put into words."
                                                        —E. H. Gombrich[1]

As I indicated earlier, because *Cymbeline*, *The Winter's Tale*, and
The Tempest are open form dramas, their meanings are absolutely
contingent on their dramaturgy. The double view of life as both
comic and tragic, with all that this double view entails, grows out of
the blending of tragedy and comedy in the Romances; the double view
of artistic creations and of the appearance we take for reality, or the
reality which sometimes seems illusory, is the result of the conflating
of representational and presentational styles; the simultaneous awareness of "life as drama" (immediate, active, present) and "life as
tale" (mediated by the teller, distanced, fixed in past time) results
from the juxtaposition of narrative and dramatic modes. In choosing
genre, style, mode, Shakespeare confronts a form with its opposite,
using each form as a channel of perception;[2] he thus forces us to
question all representations of reality (all partial tragic or comic
views, all dramatic constructs which play upon our willingness to
suspend disbelief, all spectacles which are "really" only gauze and
tinsel); we are then led to question the reality of the empirical world
itself (as actions which purport to be real, and in which we feel involved, are revealed as fictions—just a tale for a winter evening, or
the enchantment of a magician); and, finally, illusion becomes
equated with dream, magic, and those very stage representations of
life which have already been revealed as fraudulent. At this point,

lines separating substance and semblance begin to blur: that which seems to us most real (death, for instance) is revealed as illusory, and illusions (like Hermione's statue) become warm and breathe.

As the levels of stage play, real life, and dream-vision are reduced (or raised) to one, certain constants in the Shakespearean world and the real world appear in a new and unaccustomed light. Death, for example, is freed from its tragic connotations and is allowed to enter and become a central part of the Romance world. Each of the three plays is permeated by death. Yet, as in Greek Romance, death, though ever-present, is an elusive phenomenon. Often the death is not real, or the body, or blood, that of someone other; when the death *is* real, it is presented as casual or grotesque, one of the things that happen to people in a universe that refuses to take man seriously. Mamillius dies because Jove is angry and disappears with scarcely a gap to show where he had been in the fabric of the play's life. Antigonus, too, dies in an absurdly meaningless way: a bear is hungry and little cares that Antigonus is "a nobleman." A whole shipload of Sicilian sailors is casually devoured by the sea. And Guiderius, in his killing of Cloten, reminds us in some ways of the angry Jove or the hungry bear: no murderer, but a natural force striking out in innocent savagery, delighting in his strength and in his discovery that the decapitated head is "an empty purse" with no brains in it.

More intriguing than the casual intrusions of sudden death into the worlds of these plays are the deaths which are illusory. These pseudodeaths, and the characters' reactions to them, illustrate strikingly the discontinuity of theme which parallels the discontinuity of dramatic structure in the Romances. The "deaths" of Imogen, Posthumus, Hermione, Ferdinand, Alonso, and Prospero are intensely "real" to those who have reason to think them dead; the "deaths" serve as impetus for significant response—deep repentance, grief, attempted suicide—and call forth, as well, dirges which allay passion by speaking movingly and thoughtfully about death—death as rest from life's enormities and death as transformation into "something rich and strange." The discontinuity between the facts (which tell us that the deaths are not "real") and the characters' responses to the deaths releases us from deep involvement in the expressed grief, isolates the meditations on death and the emotions occasioned by death, and holds up these meditations and emotions for our contemplation.

Such discontinuity of theme is characteristic of these open form Romances. Contrast for a moment Shakespeare's use of death in *The Tempest* and in *Measure for Measure*. In *Measure for Measure*, a closed form tragicomedy, questions about death recur constantly. The action can even be viewed as turning on the two central questions: 1) shall Claudio die? and 2) shall Angelo die for Claudio's death? Within the action, we find a continuing debate on the philosophical question of what it means to die. And, as in the Romances, we find throughout characters who mistakenly believe—with good reason—that a character is dead. Yet questions and attitudes about death in *Measure for Measure* are an integral part of the dramatic conflict in a way that is not true of *The Tempest*, in spite of the centrality of the death theme in the Romance. In *Measure for Measure* Claudio's meditation on death is not an isolated aria, but a desperate attempt to sway Isabella; Isabella's plea for Angelo's life, set in the context of her belief that Claudio is dead, is a moving, intense, dramatic moment. Statements, questions, beliefs about death are used dynamically, as foci of dramatic struggles.

In *The Tempest*, in contrast, despite the emphasis on drowning, bereavement, and attempted murder, death is rather the occasion for response than the center of conflict. In *The Tempest*, characters do not enter into debates about death, because death, no longer under human control, is no longer a matter for debate. "What care these roarers for the name of king?" asks the boatswain. Death seems a function of a world of Nature outside of man. "The powers" incense "the sea and shores, yea, all the creatures" against sinful men; the sea changes all that is mortal in man (all that "doth fade") into coral and pearl; elemental spirits interrupt and make attempted murder seem ludicrous, as if to suggest that even the giving of death is no longer a human possibility. In these open form Romances, one loses, one grieves, and perhaps, one finds again. The death is, for a time, real; then a curtain is pulled back, and the father, seeing his son miraculously restored, can only say "If this prove / A vision of the island, one dear son / Shall I twice lose."

Compare the functions of the speeches on death-as-sleep in *Measure for Measure* and in *The Tempest*. Duke Vincentio says of life: "Thy best of rest is sleep, / And that thou oft provok'st; yet grossly fear'st / Thy death, which is no more" (*Measure for Measure* 3.1. 17–19); Prospero says of life: "We are such stuff / As dreams are made on, and our little life / Is rounded with a sleep" (*The Tempest* 4.1.156–158). Both say that death is sleep. Yet Duke Vincentio's speech functions as a part of a deliberate attempt to persuade Claudio to a new understanding of life and death, to make him "absolute for death." In contrast, Prospero seems hardly to be talking to Ferdinand at all; rather, he responds to the fading of the revels and to Ferdinand's agitation by meditating aloud on the dream-quality of life (dreams made from the same "stuff" as those in *Cymbeline:* "a bolt of nothing, shot at nothing, / Which the brain makes of fumes") and on the sleep/death into which that dream/life fades. While the speech in *Measure for Measure* is an integral part of the on going dramatic action, Prospero's speech has so little impact on the action that some have suggested that it is almost a lovely excrescence—a self-indulgence on the part of Shakespeare the poet.

Yet Prospero's speech is far from an excrescence. If the play were one in which dramatic intensity and coherence were paramount, such an aria might well be at best an ornamental flourish; here it is part of the very fabric of the play. Events happen, characters comment on them, the events fade and new events occur. Variety of event, power of response to the event—these are far more important than ongoing action or sustained dramatic conflict. Because of the chosen dramatic form, "the ear is not thrown forward into the future . . .; it is kept sternly in the present moment."[3] And, as we see in Shakespeare's handling of thematic material in his Romances, the "present moment" gains its intensity by concentration on present emotion, present belief, present vision. The breaking of constricting dramatic patterns allows such presentness and such intensity.

Character presentation, too, has an air of discontinuity in these plays, paralleling the thematic and structural discontinuities of open form drama. It makes little sense to try to come to terms with the "real" Posthumus or Leontes (or even Prospero), for these characters are often little more than a succession of masks. They are not so much "complex" as they are "various," nor are we encouraged by the plays to see them as heroes consciously living out their destinies. Hamlet, the most "various" of the tragic heroes, is presented to us as a young man with a clear sense of himself; many of his internal struggles center on the discrepancy between what he expects of himself and what his actions indicate to him that he is. In contrast, Prospero—the most "coherent" of the Romance heroes—functions in a variety of capacities in his world, adapting easily to his many roles. In him seems to be no attempt to achieve selfhood, to behave in a way befitting a preconceived self-image. Rather, he becomes easily what each situation demands, whether it be a magus, a loving father, a stage manager, or an actor begging for applause.[4]

This slipping into and out of a variety of roles is obvious in the characters of Posthumus, Cloten, Leontes, Polixenes. Whichever character we focus on, we come away convinced that we are here faced with a new kind of Shakespearean character, and, as a consequence, a new presentation of human personality. Role-playing in the Romances is not simply a part of life (as in many of the comedies), a possible way of viewing life (as in *Richard II*), nor a way of manipulating life (as with Richard III, Iago, or Edmund), but is, rather, human life itself. Life becomes here a series of roles, with the significance of that fact heightened by careful use of costume changes. One need hardly comment on the symbolic effect of the costuming of Prospero (as he changes from magician to narrator to duke), of Posthumus (who accompanies every role change with a costume change), or even of Perdita, a "real" princess who thinks herself a shepherdess but who blushingly dresses as a princess for the sheep-shearing festival. However, the transformation of Autolycus is worth noting: when he exchanges clothes with Florizel, he becomes, in the eyes of the shepherd and his son, a "gentleman" and we sense that the clothes *do* change him—instead of picking pockets, he now "picks his teeth" like a gentleman, and terrifies the two desperate men in a most courtly way.

The distinction between character presented as integral (if various) self and character as role is basic. If character is presented in the drama as self, our concern is with the growths and subtle changes in that self, with the motivations behind actions, with the confrontations of self with self as presented through dialogue and gesture. If character is a succession of roles, our interest is primarily in the story in which these roles are played out. Posthumus is intensely, murderously jealous; what function will this have in the story? (Contrast this with our attitude to Othello: when jealousy strikes the Moor, we are at least as concerned with the transformation this causes in Othello as we are in the effect on others in the play.) Posthumus is now desperately repentant; what effect will this have on the story?

(Again, contrast with *Othello*, where Othello's repentance is the final revelation of a self who is great of heart, and about whose fate we are deeply concerned.) With Posthumus, we are not told—nor do we care—what brought about the repentance, or what has happened to him since we last saw him in the role of the madly jealous husband. Because the open form dramaturgy encourages concentration on story rather than on character, event and response and succeeding event are primary, and details of motivation and change are tertiary at most. Goals and aspirations, too, are given short shrift. Hamlet dreams of cleansing Denmark, Othello of living nobly with his "fair warrior," Macbeth of being a king "uncabinned, unconfined," Lear of placing his life on Cordelia's kind nursery as he crawls unburdened toward death. As spectators we become caught up in the dreams of these heroes and feel with them the agony of all that frustrates the dream. Not so in the Romances, where events succeed one another so that, although dreams are fulfilled, these dreams do not function openly as goals. Where aspirations exist in the Romances, they are not expressed; were they expressed, they would be nostalgic—a wish for past happiness, for a time before the winds of passion or fortune brought new roles and new unhappiness.

Thematic discontinuities, character dislocations, separations of speech from action, of emotional expression from character and from the "facts"—these are characteristic of the Romances, in keeping with the plays' dramaturgy. It is impossible to identify what was the cause and what the fortunate effect in the design and construction of these plays. It is quite possible that Shakespeare felt that he had carried closed form dramaturgy to a variety of perfections, and, as a result, became interested in trying to create a new kind of dramatic experience. The masque, as open form drama, was perhaps interestingly suggestive; or perhaps an early sketch of *Pericles* offered itself as a form not governed by a comic or tragic genre, blending direct confrontation of the audience with lifelike and gripping representation, combining the powers of narrative and drama: Shakespeare may well have seen the appeal of such an interesting dramatic experiment and then have realized its power to make a new statement about life.

Or, equally plausible, a renewed interest in the fascination of Greek Romance (again, perhaps, through the discovery of *Pericles*) could well have led Shakespeare to the form of his Romances. These prose-romances present a unique and intriguing view of human life —of semihelpless man whirred by the winds of fate, yet somehow glorious in his capacities for tenacity, faith, and patience; of life as deadly serious but always fading in intensity through the effect of time. To capture that view, Shakespeare needed a new form, one comparable to the mixed form of *Pericles* and of Greek Romance. This we have in the open form of the Romances.

Or perhaps Shakespeare first of all wanted to say something about life that he had only hinted at before. This "something" had to do with man's relationship with a mysterious supernatural world, an unconcerned natural world, man's own passions and his functions in society. It had to do with "apparent" reality and "real" illusion, with the fact that one cannot predict, cannot know the truth of that which most moves him, can never know exactly what forces control him and his universe. This "something" had to do, also, with certain "truths" about fictional creations and concomitant truths about levels of reality: the level of story and stage play, the level of waking reality, and the level of dream (both actual dream and human imaginative constructs which take into account the mysterious and the nontangible.) Wanting to present something more "total" than the closed world of tragedy or comedy, of society-focused history or tragicomedy, Shakespeare may well have broken his own forms, refused any longer to present the inevitability of tragedy or the implausible delightfulness of comedy, and have given us the new profundity and the new playfulness of open form Romance. On this level, the Romances we have been considering move far beyond *Pericles*, with its much less complex view of life.

But whatever first led Shakespeare to create the worlds of *Cymbeline*, *The Winter's Tale*, and *The Tempest*, the fact remains that these most implausible, most farfetched, most unlikely of his plays are in many ways—as David Young and others have recently noted—Shakespeare's most mature reflections on art, on his own being as an artist, and on life itself. Few of us can see life consistently as tragic or as comic; few of us consistently suspend our disbelief in the face of created illusion; few can consistently give credence to a single knowable force which shapes our lives. We are thus in need of such plays as Shakespeare's Romances—plays which speak to our condition by acknowledging the contrarieties of mood, of belief and disbelief, of the nature of the human story. All of Shakespeare's plays acknowledge—at least in passing—the contrarieties and mysteries of life. But only when Shakespeare combines Greek Romance story with open form dramaturgy does he present life in its full complexity —tragic and comic, wonderful and terrible, real and unreal, and as unfathomable as Bottom's dream—and force us, through the dramatic experience, to acknowledge and experience it as such.

APPENDIX A

Aesthetic Distance and Dramatic Illusion

When we talk about "aesthetic distance" and "aesthetic response" in connection with drama, we are talking about what happens to us in the theater. The terms are used freely; hardly does one pick up an article or book about Shakespeare's Romances, for example, without finding the words *distance* or *distancing device* used often, and as if there were common understanding of the terms and of what they imply. Yet the situation is much more complex than most critics imagine.

The complexities grow out of two assumptions, each of which has its own complications. First is the assumption that we all know what we mean by "aesthetic distance." Second is the two-fold assumption that drama is indeed an aesthetic object—an art form designed for aesthetic enjoyment—and that there exists an "aesthetic experience" which is enjoyed only under certain conditions.

The fallacy behind the first assumption is that the concept of "aesthetic distance" was introduced into aesthetic theory independently by two philosophers, each of whom had his own carefully elaborated definition of the term. Edward Bullough, writing in the *British Journal of Psychology* in 1912–1913, equates "aesthetic distance" with "psychical distance" ("Psychical Distance as a Factor in Art and an Aesthetic Principle," reprinted in his *Aesthetics: Lectures and Essays*, ed. Elizabeth M. Wilkinson, Stanford, Calif.: Stanford University Press, 1957, pp. 91–130); José Ortega y Gasset sees "aesthetic distance" as "emotional distance" from the art object ("The Dehumanization of Art," trans. Helene Weyl, New York: Peter Smith, 1951; originally printed as *La Deshumanizacion del arte* in

Madrid, 1925). The differences between the two theories are large, and nowhere do they show up more flagrantly than when the philosophers turn to drama. For Ortega, aesthetic distance is hardly possible for drama; the properly distanced observer, for Ortega, ignores totally the "subject" of the art work and concentrates entirely on the form. When the spectator is aware of the "lived reality" imitated in the art work, he is carried away by his emotions; " 'lived' realities are too overpowering not to evoke a sympathy which prevents us from perceiving them in their objective purity" (pp. 26–27). Instead of delighting in the form, we delight in our own emotion—tears and laughter, which "are, aesthetically, frauds" (pp. 26–27). Hence, the artist should remove all human elements from his art—a task difficult to accomplish in drama. Even Pirandello's *Six Characters in Search of an Author*, which Ortega admires for its disruptions and dislocations of normal human personality, tends to affect us emotionally, as Ortega admits with regret. (p. 39).

When a critic like Alan R. Thompson, then, claims that the theory of aesthetic distance is "better suited to painting than to drama" in that true enjoyment of drama comes not through attention to form, but through participating in the illusion, in the story (*The Anatomy of Drama*, Berkeley: University of California Press, 1942, p. 97), he means by aesthetic distance something quite different from a critic who has been influenced by Edward Bullough. For Bullough, the aesthetic response *is* an emotional response—an imaginative participation in the illusion—but it is a "distanced" response in that it does not involve the spectator as an ego, as a participating or personally threatened self. For Bullough, art is a revelation because it shows us "things from a usually unnoticed side: that aspect of the thing which does not touch us immediately and practically." Bullough's ideal spectator is kept within the "antinomy of distance," balanced between empathy and detachment, drawn toward the human content of the story, painting, or statuary, yet distanced by the artistry of the art work. He is not emotionally distanced; rather, his emotions are, for the moment, transformed qualitatively.

The work of Harold Osborne ("The Quality of Feeling in Art," *British Journal of Aesthetics* 3, 1963: 39–53) is helpful here. In Osborne's terms, the aesthetic observer does not "perceive emotion-ally"—i.e., he does not apprehend the thing perceived "in terms of the significance it bears for him" but rather contemplates it as itself. When he perceives a design as sinister or mysterious, he does not respond as if to the implication that he is in danger from it or as if he must himself discover its secret. Rather, he savors and enjoys "the qualities it has of being sinister or mysterious. When spontaneous practical concern is held in abeyance" (Bullough's definition of the aesthetic response) "the close fusion of mood and object which is characteristic of emotional perceiving is disrupted and the mood-implications of the object are enjoyed without the vicissitudes of the mood experience." The anger of the angry man on stage is not directed at the spectator; hence, the spectator can, with aesthetic detachment, contemplate the anger, its causes, its meanings, its effects. In more concrete terms (to quote from John Gassner's *Form and Idea in Modern Theatre*, New York: Dryden Press, 1956), "When aesthetic distance has been established at a performance of *Hamlet*, I may feel the death of Hamlet deeply, and tragically, but I do not feel it with the immediacy (or, if you like, reality) that would make me want to run up onto the stage and administer first aid" (p. 211).

For Bullough, the closer our emotional involvement with the hu-man content of the art object, the better—so long as "distance" is not destroyed. Once we lose distance, the emotional quality changes, and we feel personally threatened, grieved, or uncomfortable, and we cease to experience the art object as a separate entity. Drama, for

Bullough, has built-in qualities which encourage the proper distance limits: human actors and stories with which to identify; the mechanics of the theater to remind us that what we are watching is a fiction. For those who follow Bullough, then, "aesthetic distance" is not only applicable to drama, but is an extremely important dramatic concept: it is "distance," in his sense, that separates tragedy from melodrama; it is "overdistancing" in his sense, that explains the reaction of Theseus and Hippolyta to the ludicrously "theatrical" performance of "Pyramus and Thisbe"; "underdistancing," in his sense, the reaction of Claudius to Hamlet's "Mousetrap" play.

For Edward Bullough, then, theatrical "distancing devices"—stylization, theatricality, reminders that "this is only a play"—are sometimes necessary in order to prevent the ever-present threat of underdistancing. As Maynard Mack has carefully demonstrated, Shakespeare used such devices with great skill throughout his career in order to provide the proper distance limits, the most famous example being the comment in *Twelfth Night:* "If this were play'd upon a stage now, I could condemn it as an improbable fiction"—a comment which is necessary to prevent overconcern for the plight of Malvolio. In *Hamlet,* a play much concerned with "actions that a man might play," the functioning of "aesthetic distance" (in Bullough's sense) is explored from every angle: the player's Hecuba speech, for example, is overdistanced for the theater audience through the use of highly rhetorical, florid language, in order to distinguish the playacting from the "reality" of the Hamlet action; the speech, though, moves Hamlet (though he remains distanced enough to marvel at the player's involvement in his role) and moves the actor himself to tears. "The Murder of Gonzago" is, again, overdistanced for the theater audience (again through stylization) in order to distinguish it from the "real" play; it is necessarily overdistanced for Hamlet and Horatio, who have a practical interest in the effect of the play on Claudius. But for Claudius, as I noted earlier, the play-within-the-play is underdistanced: he identifies so closely with the situation enacted that he cannot maintain the necessary detachment and must fly from the "theater," demanding light.

For Bullough, one danger that the dramatist faces is that, in his attempts to provide the necessary detachment for the audience, he may overdistance the play—may call attention so to the artificiality of the work that story interest is lost. Again, Shakespeare provides the perfect playful treatment of this subject. In the "Pyramus" segment of *A Midsummer Night's Dream*, overinflated writing, bad acting, obtrusive theatrical props, naive remarks addressed to the spectators, all serve to turn the tragical history into a farce: serve so to over-distance Theseus and his court that they can only be alternately amused and bored by the spectacle. "This is the silliest stuff that ever I heard," complains Hippolyta about a story that, were it played "straight," would rival *Romeo and Juliet* in effect.

For Ortega and his followers, such overdistancing is precisely what the dramatist should seek: for Ortega, "distance" is the same as Bullough's "overdistance." To remain within the antinomy of distance, caught up in the story so that it seems to one in its own way "real," is anathema for Ortega, Brecht, Pirandello, Genet, the Living Theater, and the "actualists" (for the term "actualist," see Richard Schechner, *Theatre Quarterly* 1, no. 2 [1971]: 50–66). For Brecht, distance limits *must* be broken so that the audience remains in full possession of their senses, aware always of the message of the play; for the "actualists," distance must disappear so that the audience may share the same environment as the actor and all distinctions between stage and audience dissolve. This brings us to the second assumption implied by the terms "aesthetic distance" and "aesthetic response": namely, that drama is an art form and that its purpose is to produce for the audience an experience that one might validly call "aesthetic."

The attacks on this assumption are, as I noted, twofold. Many doubt the validity (or the significance) of an "aesthetic experience," as defined by either Bullough or Ortega. To contemplate the "pure form" of an art object, or to disengage one's awareness from one's own person and submerge it in an art object separate from the observer is, for some thinkers, fraudulent, cheap, or impossible. Others, though admitting that a painting, ballet, or statuary might call forth this mysterious "aesthetic response" (described beautifully by Aquinas, Coleridge, Joyce, and hence in no need of repetition here), would claim that drama is *not* aesthetic in that sense; it is an experience that grew out of ritual and should return to ritual (see Antonin Artaud, the Living Theater, etc.)— or it is a medium for imparting ideas, for showing us the truth about the world. For the "ritualists" and "actualists," on the one hand, underdistancing is imperative; the audience must become an active part of the play experience. For the Brechtians, on the other hand, overdistancing is essential; signs, sudden spectacle, obtrusive music, constant reminders of fictionality, must jar the spectator out of his narcosis, and teach him that the tears of Mother Courage are ridiculous—that the point of the play is not to make us share her suffering, but to demonstrate "das rein merkantile Wesen des Kriegs."

Ironically, the greatest dramatists who would create representational or mimetic drama (to use Schechner's term), or who would create "actuals," or who would opt for Brecht's *Verfremdungseffekt* are, in every case, reaching for "reality" or for "real experience." For the Living Theater, the experience is "real" only if it actually happens to the spectator/participant; the dramatic experience is co-extensive with the real-life experience, and is "real" insofar as it is spontaneous, "lived," in no way distinct from life experiences. For the Brechtian, "reality" is "out there"; the only "real" thing about the fiction onstage is that it is a mirror reflection of what the world is; it must be a "true" reflection, and it must constantly remind us that it is an image, not the "thing itself." The creator of mimetic, representational drama, in contrast, believes in the power of audience imagination to pierce through the fictions which are presented as if real; such a dramatist creates a fictional world which the audience enters imaginatively, identifying with the characters, yet physically and personally "safe" in his theater seat and within the proper antinomy of distance. This, for the mimetic dramatist, is "reality" in its own way; the mirror is a magic mirror through which we enter with our imaginations, and from which we exit with regret, for the mirror gate leads to a golden world while ours is brazen. For Brecht or for Artaud, ever to enter that world is to be taken in by cruel deception; for Shakespeare, that world is as real, and as unreal, as the one made by Great Creating Nature—and to follow his career from his earliest to his latest plays is to see him find greater and greater confidence in the power, the "reality," of the fictions created by human imagination. Shakespeare's attitude toward his audience and toward his material was, in his last plays, so supremely confident that he could move at ease from one distance level to another, no longer imploring his audience to piece out his artificial display with its imagination (as he had done in the prologue and choruses of *Henry V*, c. 1599), but as certain as is Prospero that all is under his control, since improbable fictions, strange blends of language, magic, and supernatural interventions are all to the imagination "real."

What happens to us in the theater, then, depends very much on how the author feels about "reality," "illusion," and "aesthetic distance," and on whether the director and actors can translate for us the author's signals. Our experience may be cool and distanced, as the work is stylized, or is interrupted by obtrusive theatricality; it may be frightening, disturbing, or life-shaking, as the stage reaches out to include us physically in the work; or it may be enchanting, as our imaginations and emotions are fully engaged in larger-than-life creations. It seems to me fruitless to argue about which of these forms is "real drama"; on what grounds, other than preference, can one argue? But that all forms are in some way affected by concepts of "distance" seems unmistakable.

APPENDIX B

Brief Notes on Greek Romance

1. ELIZABETHAN TRANSLATIONS OF GREEK ROMANCES

Of the six or seven Greek Romances now extant, three were easily available to the Elizabethan public in English (as well as French and Latin) translations. The most popular, Heliodorus's *Aethiopica* (c. third century A.D.), was first "Englished" by Thomas Underdowne in c. 1569; his translation was reprinted (revised and augmented) in 1577, reprinted again in 1587, revised and reprinted in 1605, reprinted again in 1606, etc. The second, the "most delectable and pleasant history of *Clitophon and Leucippe*" by Achilles Tatius (c. third century A.D.) was translated into English by W. B(urton) in 1597 and again by Anthony Hodges in 1638. These two romances are described by Ben Edwin Perry, *The Ancient Romances* (Berkeley: University of California Press, 1967), as typical of the sophisticated Greek Romances of love and adventure: complex—indeed contorted —in structure, dependent on surprise, suspense, numerous *dei ex machina;* filled with dream-visions and oracles and magic; much emphasis on chastity, a miraculous happy ending, and a realization on the part of the characters that they are pawns in the hands of fate.

The third Greek Romance translated into English before 1640 was the Angell Daye translation of Amyot's French version of *Daphnis and Chloe* by Longus (second to fourth centuries A.D.), unique among extant Greek Romances in its pastoral emphasis and its omission of travel adventures. Unlike the *Aetheopica* and *Clitophon and Leucippe, Daphnis and Chloe* does not emphasize chastity as a primary virtue, and the structure of the novel is fairly simple, though there are the usual recognition scenes and miraculous happy endings. This work was translated into English in 1587; the next English edition was in 1656.

For the classic study of Greek Romance during the Elizabethan period, see Samuel Lee Wolff, *The Greek Romances in Elizabethan Prose Fiction* (New York: Columbia University Press, 1912). The more recent study of the Romances by Ben Edwin Perry (noted above) gives an excellent account of the early Romances (some of which were not discovered until the eighteenth century). Mr. Perry focuses on the origin and nature of Greek Romance, bringing up to date the scholarship on the dating and the nature of the various extant Romances. Of most interest to me is the fact that the very Romances easily available to Shakespeare are those most like Shakespeare's own Romances; the ones discovered later (but written earlier) are simpler, depend less on surprise and suspense, appeal more, as Perry says, to our contemplative faculties rather than to our faculty for enjoyment, wonder, and surprise.

A second note of interest is that the very flaws which even sympathetic critics find in *Cymbeline* are in fact the distinguishing characteristics of the Romances of Heliodorus and Achilles Tatius. Howard Felperin, for example, sees *Cymbeline* as "history . . . conflated with romance," "a play which ignores or betrays the principle of history, the reality principle of the brazen world. By conforming its historical action to the pattern of romance, that historical action loses all value as critique or corrective to a romance world all too easily dismissed as too good to be true" (*Shakespearean Romance*, p. 196). The conforming of history to romance, the deliberate fictiveness of the work, the use of an outer historiographical form to carry an inner dramatic substance are, according to Perry (*The Ancient Romances*, p. 148), the characteristics of sophisticated Greek Romance. The writers of Greek romance were not attempting a mimetic account of history or of the real world; they used pseudo-history, dramatic characters, conflicts and reunions, to create a particular kind of art form (see Perry, p. 38). Shakespeare, in his Romances—and most obviously in *Cymbeline*—uses pseudohistorical action, love, adventure, and magic, to create a comparable art form.

2. *CYMBELINE* 4.2
AND *CLITOPHON AND LEUCIPPE*

Much that is puzzling about the Romances (and especially about *Cymbeline*) is made understandable in the light of such sophisticated (and, according to Perry, intentionally parodistic) Greek Romances as *Clitophon and Leucippe*. Compare Imogen's lament over the headless corpse of Cloten

> O Posthumus! alas,
> Where is thy head? Where's that? Ay me! Where's that?
> Pisanio might have kill'd thee at the heart
> And left this head on.　　(4.2.320–323)

and her later gesture of embracing the bloody neck ("Give colour to my pale cheeks with thy blood" [falling on the body]), with Clitophon's lament over the headless body of a girl he thinks is Leucippe —a lament which curses Fortune for leaving him "the poor reliques of her body" and giving to the sea her head, and which ends with "but although Fortune hath dealt so with me that I cannot kisse thy lippes, yet I will kiss thy throate" (book 5, p. 11) and his earlier lament over the supposedly disemboweled Leucippe:

> Here do thy wretched corps lye, but where are thy entrailes? If they had been burnt with fire, I should have thought the misfortune a great deale the lesse; but since their sepulchre is the ravening guts of the thieves, what misfortune can be com-

pared to this mishap (O cruell aulter; O kind of meate never heard of before: could the goddes beholde such sacrifices from heaven, and not consume them with fire?)

> (*The Loves of Clitophon and Leucippe, Translated from the Greek of Achilles Tatius by William Burton, Reprinted for the first time from a copy now unique printed by Thomas Creede in 1597*, ed. Stephen Gaselee and H. F. B. Brett-Smith, New York: Bernard Gilbert Guerney, 1923, book 3, p. 16)

Notes

PROLOGUE

1. Edwards, "Shakespeare's Romances: 1900–1957," *Shakespeare Survey* 11 (1958): 18. Mr. Edwards's survey of a half-century of criticism of the Romances provides an excellent introduction to the problems confronting the critic of these plays. For another splendid review of the criticism, see Howard Felperin's "Bibliographical Appendix" in his *Shakespearean Romance* (Princeton, N.J.: Princeton University Press, 1972), pp. 287ff.

2. Frye, *A Natural Perspective: The Development of Shakespearean Comedy and Romance* (New York: Columbia University Press, 1965), pp. 27–28.

3. On the problem of the text and the authorship of *Pericles*, see, e.g., Philip Edwards, "An Approach to the Problem of *Pericles*," *Shakespeare Survey* 5 (1952): 25–49; Kenneth Muir, "Shakespeare's Hand in *Pericles*," *Shakespeare as Collaborator* (London: Methuen, 1960), pp. 56–76.

4. See Appendix B, "Brief Notes on Greek Romance"; and Carol Gesner, *Shakespeare and the Greek Romance: A Study in Origins* (Lexington: University Press of Kentucky, 1970); L. G. Salingar, "Time and Art in Shakespeare's Romances," *Renaissance Drama* 9 (1966): 3–35; F. D. Hoeniger, "Irony and Romance in *Cymbeline*," *SEL* 2 (1962): 219–228 (esp. p. 222); Elizabeth H. Haight, *More Essays in Greek Romance* (New York: Longmans, Green, 1945), pp. 142–189.

5. Burke. "Psychology and Form" and "Lexicon Rhetoricae," *Counter-Statement*, 2d ed. (Los Altos, Calif.: Hermes, 1953), pp. 29–44, 123–183.

6. Since Philip Edwards issued his challenge in 1957, several books have appeared in answer to it. Among these are Hallett Smith, *Shakespeare's Romances: A Study of Some Ways of the Imagination* (San Marino, Calif.: Huntington Library, 1972); R. A. Foakes, *Shakespeare: The Dark Comedies to the Last Plays* (Charlottesville: University of Virginia Press, 1972); Joan Hartwig, *Shakespeare's Tragicomic Vision* (Baton Rouge: Louisiana State University Press, 1972); Douglas L. Peterson, *Time, Tide, and Tempest: A Study of Shakespeare's Romances* (San Marino, Calif.: Huntington Library, 1973). I would draw particular attention to David Young's *The Heart's Forest: A Study of Shakespeare's Pastoral Plays* (New Haven, Conn.: Yale University Press, 1972), which gives perceptive readings of *The Winter's Tale*

and *The Tempest* in the light of the pastoral tradition and to Howard Felperin's *Shakespearean Romance.*

CHAPTER I

1. McArthur, "Tragic and Comic Modes," *Criticism* 3 (1961): 45.

2. *The Winter's Tale* 4.4.189. All quotes from Shakespeare's plays are taken from the Kittredge *Complete Shakespeare* (Boston: Ginn, 1936).

3. See, e.g., Cyrus Hoy, *The Hyacinth Room: An Investigation into the Nature of Comedy, Tragedy, and Tragicomedy* (New York: Alfred C. Knopf, 1964); Northrop Frye, *A Natural Perspective: The Development of Shakespearean Comedy and Romance* (New York: Columbia University Press, 1965); Frank Kermode, *Shakespeare: The Final Plays* (London: Longmans, Green, 1963).

4. The term is applied by Norman Rabkin, *Shakespeare and the Common Understanding* (New York: Free Press, 1967), p. 220, to *The Winter's Tale*, but is, I would maintain, applicable to all three of the Romances I am here considering.

5. Tillyard proposed his argument in 1938 in *Shakespeare's Last Plays* (London: Chatto and Windus, 1938). Quotations from Tillyard are from pp. 27, 48–49 of this edition.

6. Some examples of mythic, symbolic, and Christian/theological readings of the last plays are the following: F. David Hoeniger, "The Meaning of *The Winter's Tale,*" *University of Toronto Quarterly* 20, no. 1 (October 1950): 11–26; J. A. Bryant, Jr., "Shakespeare's Allegory: *The Winter's Tale,*" *Sewanee Review* 63, no. 2 (1955): 202–222; E. A. J. Honigmann, "Secondary Sources of *The Winter's Tale,*" *Philological Quarterly* 34, no. 1 (January 1955): 27–38; Derek Traversi, *An Approach to Shakespeare,* 2d ed. (London: Sando, 1957), p. 261, and *Shakespeare: The Last Phase* (London: Hollis and Carter, 1956); S. R. Maveety, "What Shakespeare Did with *Pandosto:* An Interpretation of *The Winter's Tale,*" *Pacific Coast Studies in Shakespeare,* ed. Waldo F. McNeir and Thelma N. Greenfield (Eugene: University of Oregon Press, 1966), pp. 263–279.

7. Tillyard, *Shakespeare's Last Plays,* pp. 16–17.

8. Rabkin (*Shakespeare and the Common Understanding*) also sees the first half of *The Winter's Tale* as "tragic" (p. 220), as does William H. Matchett, to mention only two recent critics who take this approach to the play. The idea is a commonly accepted one; I isolate Tillyard's argument for comment only because he seriously analyzes the implications of the idea.

Matchett, in his "Some Dramatic Techniques in *The Winter's Tale*," *Shakespeare Survey* 22 (1969): 93–107, states that "Shakespeare's problem in *The Winter's Tale* is that of compressing a complete tragedy into the first half in order to pass through and beyond it in the second. He has to work fast, but he does work" (pp. 94–95).

9. Cf. Sir Arthur Quiller-Couch, Introduction to *The Winter's Tale* (Cambridge: Cambridge University Press, 1931), pp. xxiii, xv.

10. Throughout this chapter, I use the word *fable* in the sense of a common story line with similar characters and similar dramatic action; although such story lines came to Shakespeare from different sources (the "usurping brother" fable, e.g., came to *Hamlet* from one source and to *As You Like It* from another), the "fables" are nevertheless much alike.

11. For a discussion of the contemporary scandal sheets and domestic tragedy, see William G. Meader, *Courtship in Shakespeare* (New York: King's Crown Press, 1954), p. 51, and Madeleine Doran, *Endeavors of Art: A Study of Form in Elizabethan Drama* (Madison: University of Wisconsin Press, 1964), pp. 142–143.

12. I am here, and in the following paragraph, drawing on H. B. Charlton's *Shakespearian Tragedy* (Cambridge, Mass.: Harvard University Press, 1949), pp. 113–140.

13. Robert Greene's *Pandosto*, edited by P. G. Thomas (New York: Duffield, 1907). All quotations from *Pandosto* are taken from this edition.

14. Pierre Charron, *Of Wisdome Three Bookes*, trans. Samson Lennard (London: For Edward Blount and Will Aspley [1612?]), p. 94.

15. Peter de la Primaudaye, *The Second Part of the French Academie* (London: G. B. R. N. R. B., 1594), p. 321.

16. *The Blazon of Jealousy: A subject not written of by any heretofore*, trans. Robert Tofte (London: T. S[nodham] f. J. Busbie, 1615), pp. 16–23.

17. Hyde, *Playwriting for Elizabethans, 1600–1605* (New York: Columbia University Press, 1949), p. 158.

18. Farnham, *Shakespeare's Tragic Frontier: The World of His Final Tragedies* (Berkeley and Los Angeles: University of California Press, 1950), p. 11.

19. See, e.g., Robert Burton, *The Anatomy of Melancholy*, ed. Floyd Dell and Paul Jordan-Smith (New York: Tudor, 1938), p. 840.

20. The question of passion and its relation to guilt is discussed by Saint Thomas Aquinas, *The "Summa Theologica*," 2d rev. ed. Literally Translated by the Fathers of the English Dominican Province, vol. 6, q. 24, art. 3; vol.

7, q. 73, art. 6 (London: Burns, Oates and Washbourne, 1926). The question of madness and its relation to sin is explained in some detail by Saint Thomas in vol. 7, p. 372.

21. Puttenham, "Of Poets and Poesy," in Smith, *Elizabethan Critical Essays*, 2 vols. (Oxford: Oxford University Press, 1904), 2:19. Puttenham goes on to say: "If otherwise, then doth it breed chimeres and monsters in man's imaginations, and not only in his imaginations but also in all his ordinary actions and life which ensues."

22. As Aristotle explains it, tragedy should not deal with the suffering and downfall of a completely virtuous person, "for this is not fearful and not pitiable either, but morally shocking"; Aristotle's *Poetics*, 52b34–53a7, trans. Gerald Else, *Aristotle's Poetics: The Argument* (Cambridge: Harvard University Press, 1957), p. 364. As Else explicates this passage (p. 368): "It is *outrageous* that a thoroughly good man should fall from happiness into unhappiness, and the feeling of outrage is likely to get the better of our pity for the victim."

23. G. G. Gervinus, *Shakespeare Commentaries*, 5th ed., trans. F. E. Bunnett (London: Smith, Elder, 1892), pp. 801–817.

24. This definition of the grotesque is given by Howard C. Babb "*The Great Gatsby* and the Grotesque," *Criticism* 5 (1963): 336–337.

25. Cf. Kermode, *Shakespeare: The Final Plays*, pp. 11–12.

26. See, e.g., Cyrus Hoy, Frank Kermode, Northrop Frye, n. 3, above.

27. I note, in passing, that there exists a "calumniated wife" fable with a long ancestry, stretching back, according to Margaret Schlauch, "The Man of Law's Tale," *Sources and Analogues of Chaucer's Canterbury Tales*, ed. William F. Bryan and Germaine Dempster (Chicago: University of Chicago Press, 1951), pp. 160–161, to a "third-century Greek romance with hagiographical and theological flavoring known as the *Clementine Recognitions*." L. G. Salingar, "Time and Art in Shakespeare's Romances," *Renaissance Drama* 9 (1966): 3–35, discusses the popularity during the Middle Ages of these tales of the "sorely tried heroine" and refers to numerous studies of "la femme injustment accusée" (pp. 10–11). Tales of unjustly accused wives doubtless influenced the plays we are considering, but of these plays only *Cymbeline* follows closely the general pattern described by Margaret Schlauch. *The Winter's Tale, Much Ado about Nothing*, and *Othello* are part of this pattern only in their use of an innocent heroine unjustly accused of infidelity. When I refer to the "slandered maiden fable," then, I refer not to that plot line stemming from the *Clementine Recognitions*, but to the common

fable underlying *Othello, Much Ado about Nothing* and *The Winter's Tale*.

28. For Dr. Johnson, comedy is "such a dramatic representation of human life, as may excite mirth," *The Rambler*, no. 125, *The Yale Edition of the Works of Samuel Johnson*, vol. 4, ed. W. J. Bates and Albrecht B. Strauss (New Haven, Conn.: Yale University Press, 1969), pp. 300–301.

29. See the criticisms of the play by Heinrich Bulthaupt, W. Oechelhauser, and Rodrick Benedix, quoted in Furness, *New Variorum Edition of Much Ado about Nothing*, (Philadelphia: Lippincott, 1899), pp. 377–382.

30. Quiller-Couch, Introduction to the Cambridge edition of *Much Ado about Nothing* (1923), p. xiii.

31. This is noted by Charles Prouty, in *The Sources of "Much Ado about Nothing"* (New Haven, Conn.: Yale University Press, 1950); and by Geoffrey Bullough, *Narrative and Dramatic Sources of Shakespeare* (London: Routledge and Kegan Paul, 1958), 2:76–77.

32. R. J. Kaufmann, "Puzzling Epiphanies," *Essays in Criticism* 13 (1963): 396. This essay-review of Kermode's *Shakespeare: The Last Plays* gives very fine insight into the Romances.

33. For a comparable response to the Bohemia section, see R. A. Foakes, *Shakespeare: The Dark Comedies to the Last Plays* (Charlottesville: University Press of Virginia, 1972), p. 136.

34. William Matchett, n. 8, above, analyzes this scene carefully and cogently; although I read his essay after writing this chapter, I find that in his reading of the scene and the statue scene, we are in substantial agreement.

35. This scene is wonderfully reminiscent of more than one scene in *Clitophon and Leucippe*—scenes which, like *Cymbeline* 4.2, include serio-comic laments over a dead body mistakenly thought to be that of the loved one. See Appendix B for two examples of such scenes.

36. *Coleridge's Shakespearian Criticism*, ed. Thomas H. Raysor (Cambridge, Mass.: Harvard University Press, 1930), 1:135.

37. J. F. Danby, in *Poets on Fortune's Hill* (London: Faber and Faber, [1952]), p. 98, mentions this "distortion of tone" which so often accompanies criticism of the Romances, but attributes it to critical overanxiety about the greatness of the plays.

38. Evans, *Shakespeare's Comedies* (Oxford: Clarendon Press, 1960), p. 261.

39. Knox, *"The Tempest* and the Ancient Comic Tradition," *English Stage Comedy: English Institute Essays, 1954*, ed. W. K. Wimsatt, Jr. (New York: Columbia University Press, 1955), pp. 52–73.

40. For a more detailed study of the evil in the world of *The Tempest*, see Bertrand Evans, *Shakespeare's Comedies*, pp. 319–337.

41. Hallett Smith, too, in *Shakespeare's Romances: A Study of Some Ways of the Imagination*, sees the Romances as growing out of the tragedies and comedies. His approach to the subject is considerably different from mine.

42. See Prologue, n. 4, and Appendix B.

43. McArthur, "Tragic and Comic Modes," pp. 36–37.

44. Bloomfield, "Sir Gawain and the Green Knight: An Appraisal," *PMLA* 76 (1961): 19.

CHAPTER II

1. MacNeice, *The Collected Poems of Louis MacNeice*, ed. E. R. Dodds (New York: Oxford University Press, 1967).

2. For the generally accepted dogma of the pre-1965 period, see R. A. Foakes, "Critical Introduction to *King Henry VIII*," *The Arden Shakespeare* (Cambridge, Mass.: Harvard University Press, 1957), where one may find in full the typical dissatisfactions with the dramaturgy of the last plays (esp. pp. xxxix–xl). See also Harley Granville-Barker, *Prefaces to Shakespeare* (Princeton, N.J.: Princeton University Press, 1952), 1:459–543; Sir Arthur Quiller-Couch, *Notes on Shakespeare's Workmanship* (New York: Henry Holt, 1917), pp. 254–270; Brander Matthews, *Shakespeare as a Playwright* (New York: Charles Scribner's Sons, 1923), pp. 334–337; Frank Kermode, *Shakespeare: The Final Plays* (London: Longman's Green, 1963), pp. 39–49; Allardyce Nicoll, *Shakespeare* (London: Methuen, 1952), pp. 157–177. S. L. Bethell, in *The Winter's Tale: A Study* (London: Staples Press, 1947) argues that the dramaturgy of the Romances is deliberately crude and antiquated, so designed as to call our attention to theatricality, free us from the story, and thus focus our attention on the underlying Christian allegory.

3. Among those who have cited the deliberate theatricality of the late plays, see Barbara A. Mowat, "*Cymbeline:* Crude Dramaturgy and Aesthetic Distance," *Renaissance Papers, 1966* (Durham, N.C.: Southeastern Renaissance Conference, 1967), pp. 39–48; Arthur C. Kirsch, "*Cymbeline* and Coterie Dramaturgy," *ELH* 34, no. 3 (September 1967): 285–306; Norman Rabkin, *Shakespeare and the Common Understanding* (New York: Free Press, 1967); Joan Hartwig, *Shakespeare's Tragicomic Vision* (Baton Rouge: Louisiana State University Press, 1972); R. A. Foakes, *Shakespeare: The Dark Comedies to the Last Plays* (Charlottesville: University Press of Virginia, 1972). Since the reading of my paper on *Cymbeline* in 1966, and its

publication later that year, subsequent publications on the "crude dramaturgy" of this and other Romances have made a few of my examples appear to be redundant. However, since the major point that I am making differs from that that others have made, and since I feel that the evidence I give is necessary for my argument, I have here repeated a large part of the argument I first made in 1966.

4. Arthur Wing Pinero in his *Robert Louis Stevenson as a Dramatist* (New York: Dramatic Museum of Columbia University, 1914), pp. 42–43, explains that, in drama, "there are two parts of technic": "strategy" and "tactics." The strategy is "the general laying out of a play": in a play well-designed strategically, "the situations would be artfully arranged, the story told adroitly and with spirit." Tactics, on the other hand, is "the art of getting . . . characters on and off the stage, of conveying information to the audience, and so forth."

5. The term "representational" was introduced into dramatic theory by Alexander Bakshy, who defined as "presentational" that style of drama which is deliberately theatrical, and as "representational" that drama which attempts to create the illusion that the action onstage is occurring in a recognizably real world. As Bakshy stated it: "Let us consider first what particular forms a dramatic spectacle can assume. The main forms are two. The spectacle can be treated as a true image of life existing outside and quite independently of the theatre, which form may be called 'representational.' Or it can be treated as an image of life existing in the theatre and finding its expression in the forms of the theatre, which other form may be called 'presentational'" (*The Theatre Unbound*, London: Cecil Palmer, 1923, p. 92).

6. The seminal study of Shakespeare's interest in audience engagement and detachment is, of course, Maynard Mack's essay, "Engagement and Detachment in Shakespeare's Plays," *Essays on Shakespeare and Elizabethan Drama in Honor of Hardin Craig*, ed. Richard Hosley (Columbia: University of Missouri Press, 1962), pp. 275–296.

7. For an examination of the theory of aesthetic distance in drama, see Appendix A. Bullough's essay on "Psychical Distance as a Factor in Art and as Aesthetic Principle" was originally printed in *The British Journal of Psychology* 5 (1912–1913): 87–118, and is reprinted in his *Aesthetics: Lectures and Essays*, ed. Elizabeth M. Wilkinson (Stanford, Calif.: Stanford University Press, 1957), pp. 91–130.

8. See, e.g., Harley Granville-Barker, *Prefaces to Shakespeare*, 1: 459

(where he attacks *Cymbeline*'s "banalities of stagecraft"), and R. A. Foakes's Introduction to *King Henry VIII*, pp. xxxix–xl (where all the plays, from *Pericles to The Tempest*, are found to be "profound in the study" but very disappointing as dramatic constructs).

9. The two most famous attacks are Granville-Barker's remarks on the "banalities of stagecraft" (see n. 8, above) and Samuel Johnson's on *Cymbeline*'s "unresisting imbecility," its "faults too evident for detection, and too gross for aggravation," *Yale Edition of the Works of Samuel Johnson*, 8: 908. The scene to be analyzed in this chapter (I.5) is marked as I.6 in some editions of *Cymbeline*.

10. Muriel C. Bradbrook, *Elizabethan Stage Conditions. A Study of Their Place in the Interpretation of Shakespeare's Plays* (Hamden, Conn.: Archon Books, 1962, first printed 1932), p. 88; Samuel Johnson, *Yale Edition of the Works of Samuel Johnson*, 8: 881. As Furness noted in the Variorum *Cymbeline* (Philadelphia: Lippincott, 1913), p. 66: "Garrick omitted this soliloquy in the stage performance, for which he is thus criticized by Reed (*Biog. Dram.* iii, 149) in speaking of Garrick's *Version:* 'By omitting the physician's soliloquy, we are utterly unprepared for the recovery of Imogen after she had swallowed the potion prepared by her stepmother. To save appearances this speech was inserted in the printed copy, but was never uttered on the stage. Useless as it might be to those who are intimately acquainted with the piece, it is still necessary toward the information of a common audience.' "

11. Cf. Edgar Stoll, *Shakespeare Studies* (New York: G. E. Stechert, 1942), p. 107.

12. Horace Howard Furness, Variorum *Cymbeline*, p. 72; J. M. Nosworthy, New Arden *Cymbeline* (Cambridge, Mass.: Harvard Univ. Press, 1955), p. 32, n. 85. Furness, arguing that this "jarring tag," coming at the close of a scene of such solemnity, a scene which reveals for the first time the "desperate character of the Queen" and the "dark intimations that Imogen is to be killed by poison," must surely have been added by "the interpolator," concludes (Preface to the Variorum *Cymbeline*, p. viii): "Were this play a comedy, these lines would be well enough. They superfluously make assurance double sure. But the atmosphere is as tragic to the last scene as any down-right tragedy; there is not a comic character in it, and to give a comic turn to any speech of Pisanio, on whose weary, faithful shoulders so much of the tragedy rests, is, as it seems to me, utterly unShakespearian."

13. Cf. Anne Righter, *Shakespeare and the Idea of the Play* (London:

Chatto and Windus, 1964), pp. 20–23, for a helpful discussion of the function of audience-directed tactics in the mystery and morality plays.

14. McCollom, "Formalism and Illusion in Shakespearian Drama, 1595–1598," *The Quarterly Journal of Speech* 31 (1945), 446.

15. Morris Arnold, *The Soliloquies of Shakespeare: A Study in Technic* (New York: Columbia University Press, 1911), pp. 24–25, 44–45.

16. Coghill, *Shakespeare's Professional Skills* (Cambridge: Cambridge University Press, 1964), p. 138.

17. Warren D. Smith, in his "Shakespeare's Stagecraft as Denoted by the Dialogue in the Original Printings of His Texts" (Ph.D. diss., University of Pennsylvania, Philadelphia, 1947), pp. 142–144, discusses Shakespeare's obtrusive entrance and exit signals in his earliest plays.

18. Roemer, "The Surfaces of Reality," *Film Quarterly* 18, no. 1 (Fall 1964): 14–22.

19. George Puttenham, *The Arte of English Poesie*, 3:7, ed. Edward Arber (London: Alexander Murry and Son, 1869), p. 166; originally printed 1589.

20. Robert Langbbaum, *The Poetry of Experience* (London: Chatto and Windus, 1957), p. 83.

21. Alan R. Thompson, *The Anatomy of Drama* (Berkeley: University of California Press, 1942), pp. 96–97, notes that "the more artificial a convention is, the quicker the playgoer will be to note any departures from it, or any inexpertness in its use; and when they do, dramatic illusion is endangered."

22. J. M. Nosworthy, Introduction to the New Arden *Cymbeline*, p. xxx.

23. Harley Granville-Barker, *Prefaces to Shakespeare* 1:465.

24. This juxtaposition of language styles has been noted also by Norman Rabkin, *Shakespeare and the Common Understanding*, by F. C. Tinkler, "*Cymbeline*," *Scrutiny* 7 (1938): 5–10, and by J. P. Brockbank, "History and Histrionics in *Cymbeline*," *Shakespeare Survey* 11 (1958): 42–49.

25. Gassner, "Forms of Modern Drama," *Dramatic Soundings*, ed. Glenn Loney (New York: Crown, 1968), p. 665.

26. For an interesting analysis of the language of *The Winter's Tale*, see Frank Kermode, "Introduction to *The Winter's Tale*," Signet Classic Edition (New York: New American Library, 1963).

27. Bethell, *The Winter's Tale: A Study* (London: Staples Press, 1947), pp. 47–50.

28. Here again it is interesting to compare the use of play references to

those in an early comedy like *Love's Labours Lost*, where such references (as Northrop Frye points out, *A Natural Perspective*, p. 111) serve merely to emphasize the artificiality of the play, the mirror reflecting the mirror. In *The Winter's Tale* such references are so placed that they suddenly alter audience awareness, or are so clustered that an entire section of the play is thrown into the presentational mode. Since the play references in *The Winter's Tale* intrude into representational drama, their "artificialness" has a far different effect than the artifice of the same device in an early sophisticated comedy.

29. See Bethell, *The Winter's Tale: A Study*, pp. 51–52.

30. Introduction to the New Arden *Tempest*, ed. Frank Kermode (London: Methuen, 1954), pp. xxxiv–lxxxviii.

31. Stephen Orgel, *The Jonsonian Masque* (Cambridge, Mass.: Harvard University Press, 1965), pp. 13–14; Enid Welsford, *The Court Masque: A Study in the Relationship between Poetry and the Revels* (New York: Russell and Russell, 1962), pp. 339 ff.

32. Cf. Orgel, *The Jonsonian Masque*, pp. 13–14.

33. See E. H. Gombrich, *Art and Illusion: A Study in the Psychology of Pictorial Representation* (New York: Pantheon Books, Bollingen Series 35, no. 5, 1960), pp. 242–287.

34. See Appendix A.

35. A sensitive reading of *Cymbeline*, e.g., led to an incredibly fine and moving production of this play at Stratford, Ontario, in 1970. In the Stratford production fluctuations of dramatic style were obediently followed by director and actors with presentational moments (stylized acting, explosive spectacle, acknowledged make-believe) alternating with intense emotion and realistic conflict. According to the program notes (written by Michael Bawtree, assistant to director Jean Gascon) the strangeness of the play must be recognized by the director and the cast, since "the experimental audacity of *Cymbeline*'s writing invites the same kind of courage in those who produce it for the stage." The story, he says, "makes no attempt to be believable other than to be happening in front of our eyes. If its oddities are to be laughed at, they avoid being ridiculous because the play's participants seem to find them quite as odd as we do. It is as though the suffering characters of *King Lear* have been transported to Wonderland and then challenged mockingly to try and remain their huge, tragic selves." What was Shakespeare about? asks Bawtree. "His earlier plays show he was perfectly able, if he wished, to create people and events as real as the life they mirrored. But he seems in his later years to have become less sure that life itself was real. And if all the

world was a stage, and life but a walking shadow, then theatre was free to create its own reality. So with *Cymbeline*, as with *Pericles*, *The Winter's Tale*, and *The Tempest*, Shakespeare embarked on a last, exhilarant voyage of the imagination." For a perceptive review of this production, see Walter Kerr, *New York Times*, 23 August 1970.

CHAPTER III

1. I am here using Arthur Wing Pinero's definition of dramatic strategy as "the general laying out of a play": in a play well-designed strategically, "the situations would be artfully arranged, the story told adroitly and with spirit" (*Robert Louis Stevenson as a Dramatist*, New York: Dramatic Museum of Columbia University, 1914), pp. 42–43.

2. Beckerman, *Shakespeare at the Globe: 1599–1609* (New York: Mac-Millan, 1962), pp. 24–62.

3. Leech, "The Structure of the Last Plays," *Shakespeare Survey* 11 (1958): 19–30.

4. Beckerman, pp. 40–45; Ben Jonson, *Every Man Out of His Humour*, 3.8.101–102, in *Works*, ed. C. H. Herford and Percy and Evelyn Simpson, 11 vols. (Oxford: Clarendon Press, 1925–1952), 3:522; Bowers, "Hamlet as Minister and Scourge," *PMLA* 70 (1955): 747, n. 7; discussed also in his "Shakespeare's Art: The Point of View," in *Literary Views: Critical and Historical Essays*, ed. Carroll Camden (Chicago: University of Chicago Press, 1964), pp. 45–58.

According to the *Encyclopedia of Poetry and Poetics*, ed. Alex Preminger, Frank J. Warnke, and O. B. Hardison, Jr. (Princeton, N.J.: Princeton University Press, 1965), "The meaning currently designated by 'climax' is the point of supreme interest or intensity of any graded series of events or ideas, most commonly the crisis or turning point of a story or play, e.g. the fall of Adam in *Paradise Lost* or the murder of the king in *Macbeth*."

5. Cf. N. A. Brittin, "*The Twelfth Night* of Shakespeare and Professor Draper," *Shakespeare Quarterly* 7 (1956): 211–216.

6. Beckerman, *Shakespeare at the Globe*, pp. 48–50; Marco Mincoff, "The Structural Pattern of Shakespeare's Tragedies," *Shakespeare Survey* 3 (1950): 58–65.

7. On the killing of Polonius as the *peripeteia*, see Bowers, "Hamlet as Minister and Scourge," p. 747.

8. David William, "*The Tempest* on the Stage," *Jacobean Theatre*, Stratford-upon-Avon Studies, no. 1 (London: Edward Arnold, 1960), pp. 133–

158, sees the play's action as building throughout to Prospero's forgiveness speech in 5.1, the "resolution" of the play and also, in his terminology, its "climax."

9. Bowers, "Shakespeare's Art," p. 49.

10. Cf. Madeleine Doran, *Endeavors of Art* (Madison: University of Wisconsin Press, 1964, 1st printing 1954), pp. 18–23, 259–341; Beckerman, *Shakespeare at the Globe*, pp. 24–62. Glynne Wickham, *Early English Stages, 1300 to 1660*, vol. 2, pt. 2 (London: Routledge and Kegan Paul, 1972), pp. 170 ff., makes a major point of the attempt of Elizabethan play-makers to compress into dramatic form "lengthy romantic narrative" in his argument with E. K. Chambers about Elizabethan staging.

11. This interesting popular saint's play, printed in *The Digby Mysteries*, ed. F. J. Furnivall (London: N. Trübner, 1882, pp. 53–136) is one of the few saint's plays that remain to us from the medieval period. It is described by Arnold Williams as follows: "The story is radically romantic. . . . Its architecture fits its story: variety of incident and character, action which crosses and recrosses the Mediterranean, time covering thirty or forty years. . . . Obviously we are well embarked on the road to the romantic drama of the Elizabethan age, the sort Shakespeare gives us in *Pericles* and *The Winter's Tale*" (*The Drama of Medieval England*, East Lansing: Michigan State University Press, 1961, pp. 166–167). Howard Felperin considers plays like the Digby *Mary Magdalen* as extremely influential on Shakespeare's Romances.

12. "The Defence of Poesie," in *The Complete Works of Sir Philip Sidney*, ed. Albert Feuillerat (Cambridge: Cambridge University Press, 1923), 3:38.

13. Earlier critics did, in fact, attribute *Pericles, Cymbeline,* and *The Winter's Tale* to Shakespeare's very earliest period. Coleridge, for example, says that these plays were performed late in Shakespeare's career, "when Shakespeare's celebrity as poet and his interest no less than his influence as manager enabled him to bring forward his laid-by labors of youth" (*Coleridge's Shakespearian Criticism*, ed. Thomas Middleton Raysor, Cambridge, Mass.: Harvard University Press, 1930, 1:240).

14. Susanne K. Langer, *Feeling and Form: A Theory of Art* (New York: Charles Scribner's Sons, 1953), p. 307. I am much indebted to Miss Langer's chapter on "The Dramatic Illusion," pp. 306–325, for my own concepts of drama and narrative.

15. Ibid., p. 313.

16. Lawlor, *"Pandosto* and the Nature of Dramatic Romance," *PQ* 41 (1962): 106, 112–113. This very fine study of *The Winter's Tale* focuses on "the truth of the romance-kind": namely, that the audience is given "not a foresight of events to come—indeed, surprise must play the largest part in the final unfolding—but a foretaste of happiness which will not finally be withheld."

17. Kenneth Burke, *Counter-Statement* 2d ed. (Los Altos, Calif.: Hermes, 1953), p. 124.

18. Bertrand Evans, *Shakespeare's Comedies* (Oxford: Clarendon Press, 1960), p. 314, summarizes various critical approaches to the problem of Hermione's unexpected revival. For specific essays on this question, see, for example, Adrien Bonjour, "The Final Scene of *The Winter's Tale*," *English Studies* 33 (1952): 193–208; J. E. Bullard and W. M. Fox, *"The Winter's Tale,"* *Times Literary Supplement*, 14 March 1952, p. 189 (which argues that the play as originally written did not contain the revivification of Hermione), commented on by C. B. Purdom, in *Times Literary Supplement*, 21 March 1952, p. 205; by Richard Flatter, 4 April 1952, p. 237; by W. W. Greg, 25 April 1952, p. 281; and by E. P. Kuhl, 9 May 1952, p. 313.

19. William Matchett, "Some Dramatic Techniques in *The Winter's Tale*," *Shakespeare Survey* 22 (1969): 93–107, argues that we are, in fact, subtly prepared for the onset of Leontes' jealousy and for Mamillius's death. His argument is very interesting, but, although I find his article in general a fine study of the play, I maintain that Leontes' jealousy and Mamillius's death (though perhaps subtly prepared for) do take us by surprise, and are meant to.

20. Although many critics have noted the static quality of *The Tempest*, Rose A. Zimbardo, "Form and Disorder in *The Tempest*," *Shakespeare Quarterly* 14 (1963): 49–56, states the extreme form of this idea when she says, "There is no suspense in the play because Prospero can control future as well as present action."

21. Wilson, "Action and Symbol in *Measure for Measure* and *The Tempest*," in *Shakespeare: Modern Essays in Criticism*, ed. Leonard F. Dean (New York: Oxford University Press, 1957), p. 278.

22. For interesting discussions of the role of the narrator in various kinds of prose fiction, see Wayne C. Booth, *The Rhetoric of Fiction* (Chicago: University of Chicago Press, 1961), esp. pp. 8–20, and Robert Scholes and Robert Kellogg, *The Nature of Narrative* (New York: Oxford University Press, 1966). M. C. Bradbrook, in "Romance, Farewell! *The Tempest*,"

English Literary Renaissance 1, no. 3 (1971): 239–249, finds the narrator role of Prospero important and links it with the difficulty of transferring romance to the stage. In her reading of *The Tempest*, she comments: "Romance, the least inherently dramatic of the forms that contributed to the Elizabethan stage, was the most powerful in terms of group response and group affirmation. Shakespeare's series of romances began with *Pericles*, directly involving an archaic narrative form; he ended with a play where the narrative and its narrator, its leading figure, were identified at the opening" (p. 248).

23. Sir Arthur Quiller-Couch, *Notes on Shakespeare's Workmanship* (New York: Henry Holt, 1917), pp. 201–202; 265–266.

24. J. M. Nosworthy, "Introduction to the New Arden *Cymbeline*" (Cambridge: Harvard University Press, 1955), pp. xxx–xxxiii; xlviii; Harley Granville-Barker, *Prefaces to Shakespeare* (Princeton, N.J.: Princeton University Press, 1952), 1:461–462.

25. S. L. Bethell, *The Winter's Tale: A Study* (London: Staples Press, 1947), pp. 51–52. On Prospero's too-open explanations and interpretations, see Harold Wilson, "Action and Symbol," pp. 266, 278–279; and Bertrand Evans, *Shakespeare's Comedies*, pp. 331–337. Enid Welsford, too, in *The Court Masque* (New York: Russell and Russell, 1962; 1st published, 1927), pp. 338–349, asserts that it is "the part played by Prospero" as explainer, storyteller, revealer, that makes *The Tempest* essentially nondramatic.

26. Robert Scholes and Robert Kellogg, *The Nature of Narrative* (New York: Oxford University Press, 1966), p. 4.

27. See Aristotle's *Poetics*, trans. Gerald Else, in *Aristotle's Poetics: The Argument* (Cambridge, Mass.: Harvard University Press, 1957), p. 602, and Else's elaboration and explanation of Aristotle's comments, pp. 608–611.

28. Cf. Susanne Langer, *Feeling and Form*, pp. 261–265.

29. Carol Gesner traces out much of the similarity of structure between *Cymbeline* and the *Aethiopica* in her essay on "*Cymbeline* and the Greek Romance: A Study in Genre," *Studies in English Renaissance Literature*, ed. Waldo F. McNeir (Baton Rouge: Louisiana State University Press, 1962), pp. 105–131. See also her more recent *Shakespeare and the Greek Romance* (Lexington: University of Kentucky Press, 1970).

30. *The Ancient Romances: A Literary-Historical Account of their Origins* (Berkeley: University of California Press, 1967). The tendency of Greek Romance to use highly spectacular scenes interspersed with complex narrative threads was also pointed out by Samuel Lee Wolff, *The Greek Romances in Elizabethan Prose Fiction* (New York: Columbia University Press, 1912).

31. *Two Concepts of Allegory: A Study of Shakespeare's "The Tempest"* *and the Logic of Allegorical Expression* (London: Routledge and Kegan Paul, 1967), p. 156.

32. Northrop Frye stresses this fact in relating the romances to the comedies in *A Natural Perspective*, and Howard Felperin in *Shakespearean Romance* sees romance as the understructure of Shakespearean comedy, tragedy, and tragicomedy.

CHAPTER IV

1. For an excellent study of *Pericles*, see John Arthos, "*Pericles, Prince of Tyre:* A Study in the Dramatic Use of Romantic Narrative," *Shakespeare Quarterly* 4 (1953): 257–270, esp. pp. 262–263.

2. See, for example, Richard Schechner on "triangular" vs. "open" drama, "Approaches to Theory/Criticism," *Tulane Drama Review* 10, no. 4 (1966): 20–53; Richard Schechner on "mimetic drama" vs. "actuals," "Actuals: Primitive Ritual and Performance Theory," *Theatre Quarterly* 1, no. 2 (1971): 49–66; Marvin Rosenberg on "linear" vs. "contextual" drama, "A Metaphor for Dramatic Form," *Journal of Aesthetics and Art Criticism* 17, no. 2 (1958): 174–180.

3. A term applied to *The Tempest* by Erika Flamm, "Offener und geschlossener Dramenstil in Shakespeares *Tempest*," *Shakespeare Jahrbuch* 109 (1963): 142–160. The terms "open form" and "closed form" were introduced into art criticism by Heinrich Wölfflin, and have since often been applied to literature and drama. (Wölfflin, *Kunstgeschichtliche Grundbegriffe: Das Problem der Stilentwickelung in der neueren Kunst*, Munich, 1915; trans. M. D. Hottinger, *Principles of Art History*, London: G. Bell and Sons, 1932; reprint, New York: Dover Publications, n.d.).

4. The first scholar to pick up Wölfflin's open form–closed form *Begriffspaar* and apply it to literature was, as far as I can determine, Oskar Walzel, whose application of the terminology to literature appeared first in his "Shakespeares dramatische Baukunst," *Shakespeare Jahrbuch* 52, (1916): 3–35. Most of the German scholarship on this subject goes back to Walzel. See, e.g., Erwin Scheuer, "Akt und Szene in der offenen Form des Dramas dargestellt an den Dramen Georg Büchners," *Germanische Studien* 77 (1929); Robert Petsch, *Wesen und Formen des Dramas* (Halle: Max Niemeyer Verlag, 1945); Fritz Martini, "Robert Petsch: Wesen und Formen des Dramas. Ein Bericht über den ungedruckten zweiten Band," *Deutsche Vierteljahrschrift* 27 (1953): 289–308. For these scholars, all Shakespearean drama

is "open" as opposed to the "closed" drama of a Racine; i.e., the distinction they make is essentially that made by Prosser Hall Frye in his work *Romance and Tragedy* (Lincoln: University of Nebraska Press, 1961; 1st published, 1908)—a distinction that has more to do with the nature of the world represented in the play than it does with the dramatic form. For distinctions in some ways comparable to those that I will make, see Volker Klotz, *Geschlossene und offene Form in Drama* (Munich: Carl Hanser Verlag, 1960), and Walter Hinck, *Die Dramaturgie des späten Brecht* (Göttingen: Vandenhoeck und Ruprecht, 1966).

Another critic who has used the open-closed distinction is Robert Adams, *Strains of Discord: Studies in Literary Openness* (Ithaca, N.Y.: Cornell University Press, 1958). Adams recognizes that literary form must be treated differently than form in the plastic arts. His insights are perceptive and extremely helpful, but his definition of literary form as a "structure of meanings" makes his work complementary to rather than parallel with mine. For Adams the refusal to resolve within the work the problems raised by the work itself is the defining characteristic for open form literature; a work may be open in this sense and firmly closed dramatically as I define the term. Ibsen's middle plays, e.g., are selected by Adams as examples of literary openness on the grounds that they do not resolve the conflicting patterns of assertions made in them; in terms of open and closed form as I define it, the plays are in all other ways closed.

5. "Lexicon Rhetoricae," *Counter-Statement*, 2d ed. (Los Altos, Calif.: Hermes, 1953, 1st published, 1931), pp. 123–183. Other references to this volume of Burke's writings cite this essay or the earlier essay on "Psychology and Form," pp. 29–44. His basic statements about music, literature, and frustration of expectations will be found on pp. 31, 33, and 36. A later examination of his own concepts of literary form may be found in his "Dramatic Form—And: Tracking Down Implications," *Tulane Drama Review* 10, no. 4 (1966): 54–63.

6. Leonard B. Meyer, *Emotion and Meaning in Music* (Chicago: University of Chicago Press, 1956).

7. Susanne Langer, *Feeling and Form: A Theory of Art* (New York: Charles Scribner's Sons, 1953), pp. 214–215, makes this same point, noting that the first words of a poem "effect the break with the reader's actual environment."

8. Burke, "Lexicon," p. 125.

9. The sense of adventitiousness is the quality most stressed by Wölfflin in his analysis of open form painting—that style of painting which ignores both symmetry and the frame which bounds it. See Wölfflin, *Principles of Art History*, esp. pp. 124–126.

10. In the even more recent happenings and "actuals," the forms have been destroyed; instead of drama (which implies at least some separation between actor and audience, and, if not a script, at least some sense of plot or direction among the actors), we find unpatterned activity which includes "actors" and "audience" as a nearly unified group. See Schechner, *Theatre Quarterly* 1, no. 2 (1971): 49–66.

11. Frye, *The Modern Century* (Toronto: Oxford University Press, 1967).

12. See Bernard Beckerman, *Shakespeare at the Globe*, p. 46.

13. Cf. Flamm, "Offener und Geschlossener Dramenstil in Shakespeares *Tempest*," p. 149.

14. Ibid., p. 153. The translations of Erika Flamm's article are mine.

15. Nelson, *Play within a Play* (New Haven, Conn.: Yale University Press, 1958), p. 30.

16. Young, *The Heart's Forest* (New Haven, Conn.: Yale University Press, 1972), pp. 189–190.

17. Ibid., p. 177.

18. Cope, "The Rediscovery of Anti-Form in Renaissance Drama," *Comparative Drama* 2 (1968): 159; reprinted, with some revisions, in *The Theatre and the Dream* (Baltimore: Johns Hopkins Press, 1973), pp. 1–13.

19. Kott, *Shakespeare Our Contemporary*, trans. Boleslaw Taborski (London: Methuen, 1964; 1st published, Warsaw, Poland, 1964), p. 203. For Kott's analysis of *The Tempest*, see pp. 174–216.

20. See Oscar Büdel, *Pirandello* (New York: Hillary House, 1966), p. 36.

CHAPTER V

1. *Art and Illusion: A Study in the Psychology of Pictorial Representation* (New York: Pantheon, Bollingen Series 35, no. 5, 1960), p. 6.

2. Professor Wolfgang Iser notes the close relationship between mixed modes and controlled audience response, pointing out that conflicting sets of expectations turn the forms into channels of perception, in his article "Wirklichkeit und Form in Smolletts *Humphrey Clinker*," *Europäische Aufklärung. Herbert Dieckmann zum 60. Geburtstag*, ed. Hugo Friedrich und Fritz Schalk (Munich: Wilhelm Fink, 1966), pp. 87–115. See also Benbow Ritchie,

NOTES

"The Formal Structure of the Aesthetic Object," in *The Problems of Aesthetics*, ed. Eliseo Vivas and Murray Krieger (New York: Holt, Rinehart and Winston, 1963), pp. 225–233.

3. Northrop Frye, *The Modern Century* (New York: Oxford University Press, 1967), pp. 72–73, quoted in chap. 4 above.

4. See David Young, *The Heart's Forest*, pp. 155–162, on Prospero's "roles."

List of Works Cited

Achilles Tatius, *The Loves of Clitophon and Leucippe.* Translated by W. B[urton]. London: Thomas Creede, 1597. Reprint, edited by Stephen Gaselee and H. F. B. Brett-Smith. New York: Bernard Gilbert Guerney, 1923.

Adams, Robert M. *Strains of Discord: Studies in Literary Openness.* Ithaca, N.Y.: Cornell University Press, 1958.

Arnold, Morris LeRoy. *The Soliloquies of Shakespeare: A Study in Technic.* New York: Columbia University Press, 1911.

Arthos, John. "*Pericles, Prince of Tyre:* A Study in the Dramatic Use of Romantic Narrative." *Shakespeare Quarterly* 4 (1953): 257–270.

Babb, Howard C. "*The Great Gatsby* and the Grotesque." *Criticism* 5 (1963): 336–48.

Bakshy, Alexander. *The Theatre Unbound.* London: Cecil Palmer, 1923.

Beckerman, Bernard. *Shakespeare at the Globe: 1599–1609.* New York: Mac-Millan, 1962.

Bethell, Samuel Leslie. *The Winter's Tale: A Study.* London: Staples Press, 1947.

Bloomfield, Morton. "Sir Gawain and the Green Knight: An Appraisal." *PMLA* 76 (1961): 7–19.

Bonjour, Adrien. "The Final Scene of *The Winter's Tale.*" *English Studies* 33 (1952): 193–208.

Booth, Wayne C. *The Rhetoric of Fiction.* Chicago: University of Chicago Press, 1961.

Bowers, Fredson. "Hamlet as Minister and Scourge." *PMLA* 70 (1955): 740–749.

————. "Shakespeare's Art: The Point of View." In *Literary Views: Critical and Historical Essays.* Edited by Carroll Camden. Chicago: University of Chicago Press, 1964.

Bradbrook, Muriel C. *Elizabethan Stage Conditions. A Study of Their Place in the Interpretation of Shakespeare's Plays.* Hamden, Conn.: Archon Books, 1962. (First printed, 1932.)

————. "Romance, Farewell! *The Tempest.*" *English Literary Renaissance* 1, no. 3 (1971): 239–249.

LIST OF WORKS CITED

Brittin, N. A. "The *Twelfth Night* of Shakespeare and Professor Draper." *Shakespeare Quarterly* 7 (1956): 211–216.

Brockbank, J. P. "History and Histrionics in *Cymbeline*." *Shakespeare Survey* 11 (1958): 42–49.

Bryant, J. A., Jr. "Shakespeare's Allegory: *The Winter's Tale*." *Sewanee Review* 63, no. 2 (1955): 202–222.

Büdel, Oscar. *Pirandello*. New York: Hillary House, 1966.

Bullard, J. E., and Fox, W. M. "*The Winter's Tale*." *Times Literary Supplement*, March 14, 1952, p. 189.

Bullough, Edwtrd. *Aesthetics: Lectures and Essays*. Edited by Elizabeth M. Wilkinson. Stanford, Calif.: Stanford University Press, 1957.

Bullough, Geoffrey, ed. *Narrative and Dramatic Sources of Shakespeare*. 6 vols. London: Routledge and Kegan Paul, 1957–.

Burke, Kenneth. *Counter-Statement*. 2d ed. Los Altos, Calif.: Hermes, 1953.

————. "Dramatic Form—And: Tracking Down Implications." *Tulane Drama Review*, T 32, 10, no. 4 (1966): 54–63.

Burton, Robert. *The Anatomy of Melancholy*. Edited by Floyd Dell and Paul Jordan-Smith. New York: Tudor, 1938.

Charlton, H. B. *Shakespearian Tragedy*. Cambridge, Mass.: Harvard University Press, 1949.

Charron, Pierre. *Of Wisdome Three Bookes*. Translated by Samson Lennard. London: For Edward Blount and Will Aspley, [1612?].

Coghill, Nevill. *Shakespeare's Professional Skills*. Cambridge: Cambridge University Press, 1964.

Coleridge, Samuel Taylor. *Coleridge's Shakespearian Criticism*. Edited by Thomas M. Raysor. 2 vols. Cambridge, Mass.: Harvard University Press, 1930.

Cope, Jackson I. "The Rediscovery of Anti-form in Renaissance Drama." *Comparative Drama* 2 (1968): 155–171.

————. *The Theatre and the Dream: From Metaphor to Form in Renaissance Drama*. Baltimore: Johns Hopkins Press, 1973.

Craig, Hardin. "Shakespeare's Development as a Dramatist in the Light of his Experience." *Studies in Philology* 39 (1942): 226–238.

Danby, J. F. *Poets on Fortune's Hill*. London: Faber and Faber, [1952].

Doran, Madeleine. *Endeavors of Art: A Study of Form in Elizabethan Drama*. Madison: University of Wisconsin Press, 1964. (First printed, 1954.)

Edwards, Philip. "An Approach to the Problem of *Pericles*." *Shakespeare Survey* 5 (1952): 25–49.

————. "Shakespeare's Romances, 1900–1957." *Shakespeare Survey* 11 (1958): 1–18.

Else, Gerald. *Aristotle's Poetics: The Argument*. Cambridge: Harvard University Press, 1957.

Evans, Bertrand. *Shakespeare's Comedies*. Oxford: Clarendon Press, 1960.

Farnham, Willard. *Shakespeare's Tragic Frontier: The World of His Final Tragedies*. Berkeley and Los Angeles: University of California Press, 1950.

Felperin, Howard. *Shakespearean Romance*. Princeton, N.J.: Princeton University Press, 1972.

Flamm, Erika. "Offener und Geschlossener Dramenstil in Shakespeares *Tempest*." *Shakespeare Jahrbuch* 109 (1963): 142–160.

Foakes, R. A. *Shakespeare: The Dark Comedies to the Last Plays*. Charlottesville: University of Virginia Press, 1972.

Frye, Northrop. *A Natural Perspective: The Development of Shakespearean Comedy and Romance*. New York: Columbia University Press, 1965.

————. *The Modern Century*. Toronto: Oxford University Press, 1967.

Frye, Prosser Hall. *Romance and Tragedy: A Study of Classic and Romantic Elements in the Great Tragedies of European Literature*. Lincoln: University of Nebraska Press. A Bison Book. 1961. (First printed, 1908).

Furnivall, F. J., ed., *The Digby Mysteries*. New Shakespeare Society, ser. 7, no. 1. London: N. Trübner, 1882.

Gassner, John. *Dramatic Soundings*. Edited by Glenn Loney. New York: Crown, 1968.

————. *Form and Idea in Modern Theatre*. New York: Dryden Press, 1956.

Gervinus, G. G. *Shakespeare Commentaries*. 5th ed. Translated by F. E. Bunnett. London: Smith, Elder, 1892.

Gesner, Carol. "*Cymbeline* and the Greek Romance: A Study in Genre." In *Studies in English Renaissance Literature*. Edited by Waldo F. McNeir. Baton Rouge: Louisiana State University Press, 1962.

————. *Shakespeare and the Greek Romance: A Study in Origins*. Lexington: University Press of Kentucky, 1970.

Gombrich, E. H. *Art and Illusion: A Study in the Psychology of Pictorial Representation*. New York: Pantheon Books. Bollingen Series 35, no. 5, 1960.

Granville-Barker, Harley. *Prefaces to Shakespeare*. 2 vols. Princeton, N.J.: Princeton University Press, 1952.

Greene, Robert. *Pandosto; or, The Triumph of Time*. Edited by P. G. Thomas. New York: Duffield, 1907.

Haight, Elizabeth H. *More Essays in Greek Romance*. New York: Longmans, Green, 1945.

Hartwig, Joan. *Shakespeare's Tragicomic Vision*. Baton Rouge: Louisiana State University Press, 1972.

Heliodorus. *An Aethiopian History*. Translated by Thomas Underdowne. London: H. Wykes, [1569?]. Reprint, edition of 1587, *The Tudor Translations* no. 5. Edited by W. E. Henley. London: David Nutt, 1895.

Hinck, Walter. *Die Dramaturgie des Späten Brecht*. Göttingen: Vandenhoeck und Reprecht, 1966.

Hoeniger, F. David. "Irony and Romance in *Cymbeline*." *SEL* 2 (1962): 219–228.

————. "The Meaning of *The Winter's Tale*." *University of Toronto Quarterly* 20, no. 1 (1950): 11–26.

Honigmann, E. A. J. "Secondary Sources of *The Winter's Tale*." *Philological Quarterly* 34, no. 1 (1955): 27–38.

Hoy, Cyrus. *The Hyacinth Room: An Investigation into the Nature of Comedy, Tragedy, and Tragicomedy*. New York: Alfred C. Knopf, 1964.

Hyde, Mary Crapo. *Playwriting for Elizabethans, 1600–1605*. New York: Columbia University Press, 1949.

Iser, Wolfgang. "Wirklichkeit und Form in Smolletts *Humphrey Clinker*." In *Europäische Aufklärung. Herbert Dieckmann zum 60. Geburtstag*. Edited by Hugo Friedrich and Fritz Schalk. Munich: Wilhelm Fink, 1966.

Johnson, Samuel. *The Yale Edition of the Works of Samuel Johnson*. Edited by W. J. Bates and Albrecht B. Strauss. New Haven, Conn.: Yale University Press, 1958–.

Jonson, Ben. *Works*. Edited by C. H. Herford and Percy and Evelyn Simpson. 11 vols. Oxford: Clarendon Press, 1925–1952.

Kaufmann, R. J. "Puzzling Epiphanies: A Review of *Shakespeare: The Final Plays*, by Frank Kermode." *Essays in Criticism* 13 (1963) 392–403.

Kermode, Frank. *Shakespeare: The Final Plays*. London: Longman's, Green, 1963.

Kirsch, Arthur C. "*Cymbeline* and Coterie Dramaturgy." *ELH* 34, no. 3 (September, 1967): 285–306.

Klotz, Volker. *Geschlossene und offene Form im Drama*. Munich: Carl Hanser Verlag, 1960.

Knox, Bernard. "*The Tempest* and the Ancient Comic Tradition." In *English Stage Comedy. English Institute Essays, 1954*. Edited by W. K. Wimsatt, Jr. New York: Columbia University Press, 1955.

LIST OF WORKS CITED

Kott, Jan. *Shakespeare Our Contemporary.* Translated by Boleslaw Taborski. London: Methuen, 1964.

Langbaum, Robert. *The Poetry of Experience.* London: Chatto and Windus, 1957.

Langer, Susanne K. *Feeling and Form: A Theory of Art.* New York: Charles Scribner's Sons, 1953.

Lawlor, John. "*Pandosto* and the Nature of Dramatic Romance." *Philological Quarterly* 41 (1962): 96–113.

Leech, Clifford. "The Structure of the Last Plays." *Shakespeare Survey* 11 (1958): 19–30.

Longus. *Daphnis and Chloe.* Translated by Angell Daye. London: Robert Waldegrave, 1587. Reprint, *The Tudor Library*, no. 2. Edited by Joseph Jacobs. London: David Nutt, 1890.

McArthur, Herbert. "Tragic and Comic Modes." *Criticism* 3 (1961): 37–45.

McCollom, William G. "Formalism and Illusion in Shakespearian Drama, 1595–1598." *Quarterly Journal of Speech* 31 (1945): 446–453.

Mack, Maynard. "Engagement and Detachment in Shakespeare's Plays." In *Essays on Shakespeare and Elizabethan Drama in Honor of Hardin Craig.* Edited by Richard Hosley. Columbia: University of Missouri Press, 1962.

MacNeice, Louis. *The Collected Poems of Louis MacNeice.* Edited by E. R. Dodds. New York: Oxford University Press, 1967.

Martini, Fritz. "Robert Petsch: Wesen und Formen des Dramas. Ein Bericht über den ungedruckten zweiten Band." *Deutsche Vierteljahrschrift* 27 (1953): 289–308.

Matchett, William H. "Some Dramatic Techniques in *The Winter's Tale.*" *Shakespeare Survey* 22 (1969): 93–107.

Matthews, Brander. *Shakespeare as a Playwright.* New York: Charles Scribner's Sons, 1923.

Maveety, S. R. "What Shakespeare Did with *Pandosto:* An Interpretation of *The Winter's Tale.*" In *Pacific Coast Studies in Shakespeare.* Edited by Waldo F. McNeir and Thelma N. Greenfield. Eugene: University of Oregon Press, 1966.

Meader, William G. *Courtship in Shakespeare.* New York: King's Crown Press, 1954.

Meyer, Leonard B. *Emotion and Meaning in Music.* Chicago: University of Chicago Press, 1956.

Mincoff, Marco. "The Structural Patterns of Shakespeare's Tragedies." *Shakespeare Survey* 3 (1950): 58–65.

Mowat, Barbara A. *"Cymbeline:* Crude Dramaturgy and Aesthetic Distance." *Renaissance Papers, 1966.* Edited by George Walton Williams. Durham, N.C.: Southeastern Renaissance Conference, 1967.

Muir, Kenneth. "Shakespeare's Hand in *Pericles.*" In *Shakespeare as Collaborator.* London: Methuen, 1960.

Nelson, Robert. *Play Within a Play.* New Haven, Conn.: Yale University Press, 1958.

Nicoll, Allardyce. *Shakespeare.* London: Methuen, 1952.

Nuttall, A. D. *Two Concepts of Allegory: A Study of Shakespeare's "The Tempest" and the Logic of Allegorical Expression.* London: Routledge and Kegan Paul, 1967.

Orgel, Stephen. *The Jonsonian Masque.* Cambridge, Mass.: Harvard University Press, 1965.

Ortega y Gasset, José. *The Dehumanization of Art.* Translated by Helene Weyl. New York: Peter Smith, 1951. (Published as *La Deshumanización del arte,* Madrid, 1925.)

Osborne, Harold. "The Quality of Feeling in Art." *British Journal of Aesthetics* 3 (1963): 39–53.

Perry, Ben Edwin. *The Ancient Romances: A Literary-Historical Account of Their Origins.* Berkeley: University of California Press, 1967.

Peterson, Douglas L. *Time. Tide, and Tempest: A Study of Shakespeare's Romances.* San Marino, Calif.: The Huntington Library, 1973.

Petsch, Robert. *Wesen und Formen des Dramas.* Halle: Max Niemeyer Verlag, 1945.

Pinero, Arthur Wing. *Robert Louis Stevenson as a Dramatist.* New York: Dramatic Museum of Columbia University, 1914.

Preminger, Alex, Warnke, Frank J., and Hardison, O. B., Jr., eds. *Encyclopedia of Poetry and Poetics.* Princeton, N.J.: Princeton University Press, 1965.

Primaudaye, Peter de la. *The Second Part of the French Academie.* London: G.B.R.N.R.B., 1594.

Prouty, Charles. *The Sources of "Much Ado about Nothing."* New Haven, Conn.: Yale University Press, 1950.

Puttenham, George. *The Arte of English Poesie.* Edited by Edward Arber. London: Alexander Murray and Son, 1869.

Quiller-Couch, Sir Arthur. *Notes on Shakespeare's Workmanship.* New York: Henry Holt, 1917.

Rabkin, Norman. *Shakespeare and the Common Understanding.* New York: Free Press, 1967.

Righter, Anne. *Shakespeare and the Idea of the Play.* London: Chatto and Windus, 1964.

Ritchie, Benbow. "The Formal Structure of the Aesthetic Object." In *The Problems of Aesthetics.* Edited by Eliseo Vivas and Murray Krieger. New York: Holt, Rinehart, and Winston, 1963.

Roemer, Michael. "The Surfaces of Reality." *Film Quarterly* 18, no. 1 (1964): 14–22.

Rosenberg, Marvin. "A Metaphor for Dramatic Form." *Journal of Aesthetics and Art Criticism* 17, no. 2 (1958): 174–180.

Salingar, L. G. "Time and Art in Shakespeare's Romances." *Renaissance Drama* 9 (1966): 3–35.

Schechner, Richard. "Actuals: Primitive Ritual and Performance Theory." *Theatre Quarterly* 1, no. 2 (1971): 49–66.

———. "Approaches to Theory/Criticism." *Tulane Drama Review,* T 32, 10, no. 4 (1966): 20–53.

Scheuer, Erwin. "Akt und Szene in der offenen Form des Dramas dargestellt an den Dramas Georg Büchners." *Germanische Studien* 77 (1929).

Schlauch, Margaret. "The Man of Law's Tale." In *Sources and Analogues of Chaucer's Canterbury Tales.* Edited by William F. Bryan and Germaine Dempster. Chicago: University of Chicago Press, 1951.

Scholes, Robert, and Kellogg, Robert. *The Nature of Narrative.* New York: Oxford University Press, 1966.

Shakespeare, William. *The Complete Works.* Edited by George Lyman Kittredge. Boston: Ginn, 1936.

———. *Cymbeline.* A New Variorum Edition. Edited by Horace Howard Furness. Philadelphia: J. B. Lippincott, 1913.

———. *Cymbeline.* New Arden Edition. Edited with Introduction and notes by J. M. Nosworthy. Cambridge, Mass.: Harvard University Press, 1955.

———. *King Henry VIII.* New Arden Edition. Edited with Introduction and notes by J. M. Nosworthy. Cambridge, Mass.: Harvard University Press,

———. *Much Ado about Nothing.* A New Variorum Edition. Edited by Horace Howard Furness. Philadelphia: J. B. Lippincott, 1899.

———. *Much Ado about Nothing.* Cambridge Edition. Edited with Introduction by Sir Arthur Quiller-Couch. Cambridge: Cambridge University Press, 1923.

———. *The Tempest.* New Arden Edition. Edited with Introduction and notes by Frank Kermode. London: Methuen, 1954.

———. *The Winter's Tale.* A New Variorum Edition. Edited by Horace Howard Furness. Philadelphia: J. B. Lippincott, 1898.

———. *The Winter's Tale.* Cambridge Edition. Edited with Introduction and notes by Sir Arthur Quiller-Couch. Cambridge University Press, 1931.

———. *The Winter's Tale.* The Signet Classic Shakespeare. Edited with Introduction and notes by Frank Kermode. New York and Toronto: New American Library, 1963.

Sidney, Philip. *The Complete Works of Sir Philip Sidney.* Edited by Albert Feuillerat. 4 vols. Cambridge: Cambridge University Press, 1912–26.

Smith, G[eorge] Gregory. *Elizabethan Critical Essays.* 2 vols. London: Oxford University Press, 1904.

Smith, Hallett. *Shakespeare's Romances: A Study of Some Ways of the Imagination.* San Marino, Calif.: Huntington Library, 1972.

Smith, Warren D. "Shakespeare's Stagecraft as Denoted by the Dialogue in the Original Printings of His Texts." Dissertation, University of Pennsylvania, 1947.

Stoll, Elmer Edgar. *Art and Artifice in Shakespeare.* New York: Barnes and Noble, 1951.

———. *Shakespeare Studies: Historical and Comparative in Method.* New York: G. E. Stechert, 1942.

Thomas Aquinas, Saint. *The "Summa Theologica."* Translated by Fathers of the English Dominican Province. 2d rev. ed. 22 vols. London: Burns, Oates, and Washbourne, [1921?]–1932.

Thompson, Alan Reynolds. *The Anatomy of Drama.* Berkeley: University of California Press, 1942.

Tillyard, E. M. W. *Shakespeare's Last Plays.* London: Chatto and Windus, 1938.

Tinkler, F. C. "*Cymbeline.*" *Scrutiny* 7 (1938): 5–10.

Traversi, Derek. *An Approach to Shakespeare.* 2d ed. London: Sando, 1957.

———. *Shakespeare: The Last Phase.* London: Hollis and Carter, 1954.

Varchi, Benedetto. *The Blazon of Jealousie: a subject not written of by any heretofore.* Translated by R[obert] T[ofte]. London: T. S[nodham] for J. Busbie, 1615.

LIST OF WORKS CITED

Walzel, Oskar. "Shakespeares dramatische Baukunst." *Shakespeare Jahrbuch* 52 (1916): 3–35.

Welsford, Enid. *The Court Masque: A Study in the Relationship between Poetry and the Revels*. New York: Russell and Russell, 1962. (First published, 1927.)

Wickham, Glynne. *Early English Stages, 1300 to 1600*. 2 vols. in 3. London: Routledge and Kegan Paul, 1959–72.

William, David. "*The Tempest* on the Stage." In *Jacobean Theatre. Stratford-upon-Avon Studies*, no. 1. London: Edward Arnold, 1960.

Williams, Arnold. *The Drama of Medieval England*. East Lansing: Michigan State University Press, 1961.

Wilson, Harold S. "Action and Symbol in *Measure for Measure* and *The Tempest*." In *Shakespeare: Modern Essays in Criticism*. Edited by Leonard F. Dean. New York: Oxford University Press, 1957.

Wolff, Samuel Lee. *The Greek Romances in Elizabethan Prose Fiction*. New York: Columbia University Press, 1912.

Wölfflin, Heinrich. *Kunstgeschichtliche Grundbegriffe: Das Problem der Stilentwickelung in der neueren Kunst*. Munich, 1915. Translated by M. D. Hottinger (from the 7th German edition): *Principles of Art History*. London: G. Bell and Sons, 1932. Reprint. New York: Dover Publications, n.d.

Young, David. *The Heart's Forest: A Study of Shakespeare's Pastoral Plays*. New Haven, Conn.: Yale University Press, 1972.

Zimbardo, Rose A. "Form and Disorder in *The Tempest*." *Shakespeare Quarterly* 14 (1963): 49–56.

Index

INDEX

INDEX